ASHES TO GOLD

STORY OF A SINNER

God's Healing Power Over Addiction

DAWN M. BERGER

ASHES TO GOLD

Story of a Sinner

Copyright © 2015 by Dawn M. Berger
All rights reserved.

ISBN-13: 978-1517093259
ISBN-10: 1517093252

www.FromAshesToGold.com
Email at Dawn@FromAshesToGold.com

Cover & Book Design: Vermilion Chameleon I & D
www.vcartist.com

Printed in U.S.A

Please note that most of the names of the people in this book have been changed to protect their identities and hearts.

This book is dedicated to
Jesus, my Lord and Savior, the Blessed Virgin Mary,
and all of the lost, hurting souls in pain,
whether aware or unaware, all over the world.
If tomorrow never comes, I hope I leave behind a
testimony that points to You, Jesus. Help me to live
today as if it were my last day before entering
eternity, glorifying You and Your kingdom.
For I know not what the day may bring—I only know
I trust in You.

Unless we recover the zeal and the spirit of the first-century Christians—unless we are willing to do what they did and to pay the price that they paid—the future of our country, the days of America are numbered.

—Father John A. Hardon

Lunar Moth

Lunar moths are attracted to the moon as a source of light. In spiritual terms, they signify rebirth and new beginnings. Because they gravitate towards the light in the darkness of the night, the lunar moths are seen as a symbol of spiritual transformation, of heightened awareness, and striving towards truth.

CONTENTS

INTRODUCTION

About fifteen years ago, when I was in my mid-twenties, a close friend of mine made the statement, "Everyone has a dark side." Looking back, I had no idea at the time just how profound that statement would be to me one day. At the time, I related it to myself—for the times I was in a bad mood or got mad at someone and yelled and then felt bad afterward. I never thought of it in relation to the word evil. I never thought of myself as evil, or as having evil in me. My son loves the Star Wars movies by George Lucas. He loves to explain to me the story line and what is going on regarding the Jedi (the good side) and their fight for peace and justice against the Sith (the dark side). My son tells me, "To the Sith, what is evil is good." I find it interesting because of my fight against my own dark side. I didn't live a purposeful life on the dark side. In fact, I thought of myself as a good girl, but unknowingly, I was thinking as a Sith. My dark side was a life of sex addiction. I didn't know the way I was living my life would result in one day having such a label. There are many books about sex addiction and addiction in general by educated professionals who specialize in it. I am just a woman with a story, a woman who was solely educated by experience. Experience gives us quite an education, doesn't it? This book is not just for someone looking for answers about what sex addiction is and how to overcome it. It is a book for all people who struggle to know what their dark sides are and who need an awakening to the realization that we all have dark sides. The world isn't black and white. There are many shades of gray. Until we become aware of our dark sides and want to kill the serpent in us, we may be feeding our dark sides within without even knowing it, and all the while we view ourselves as "good"— or at least as being part of the Jedi team and not the Sith team. You can't be both. You have to pick a side. Every day we make choices, and by those choices and behaviors, we are either feeding the good side or the dark side in us. To be unaware and feed the darkness inside—darkness such as lust, avarice, or envy (some of the favorites these days, or at least the ones I used to struggle with the most)—could result in one of Satan's demons attaching to you like he did me. Then it becomes very hard to see clearly. We tend to see what is evil as good. We justify everything we do and fight against any truth that God may bring through someone, for we feel we are being judged. When I felt judged, I rebelled. God's truth often gets twisted by the dark one into judgment. God gives us free will. I am not God, and I am thankful I do not have to judge people at the end of their lives. God sees all. He has a much better view of everything from where He resides than I do. God knows our pain and why we sin. He sent His Son, Jesus, to be our Healer for those wounds, so that we no longer have to sin as a way to cope and to medicate ourselves. For that is what sin is: our way to medicate our pain. God knows this, so He sent us a Healer over two thousand years ago—a Healer who is very much here and alive today. If we seek Him, we have the illuminated key to unlock the door to this mystery called life—the mystery of why we do what we do and how we can turn back to the light. Otherwise, we stay locked in our prison cells of pain or hell. Whichever way you label it, it is after all the same. Courage is all that it takes. Do you have the courage to read this book, the courage to face your dark side, and the courage to turn to the light? If darkness and light, the notions of good and evil, and God and Satan are too much for you to comprehend, have a ten-year-old translate the Star Wars story line or watch the movies over and over again as I have done with my son. You will begin to see how easy it is to go from the good, Jedi, side to the evil, Sith, side over time due to trauma—just as Anakin Skywalker did when he became Darth Vader in Revenge of the Sith. Once you cross over, it's a fight to get back to the light. Sometimes you never realize you were wrong in the way you lived your life until the last few moments of your life are left—just as Darth Vader did, in Return of the Jedi. I think of how hard it was for Luke Skywalker in The Empire Strikes Back to realize his dad was Darth Vader. It is hard to realize our parents could have evil in them or we could have evil in us. Luke loved his dad and never gave up on him, telling his father, "There is still good in you." There is good in everyone. Let's not give up on ourselves or anyone in our lives. God doesn't, so why should we? Maybe you think it's silly for me to compare the Star Wars movies to our lives, but it was so hard for me to see my darkness, and it may be hard for you to see yours, too. Sometimes, to understand life and God, we have to become children again and see the world through the eyes of a child. As children are fresh from God and therefore closest to heaven, we can learn much from them.

One

PAIN

"Beloved, I urge you as aliens and sojourners to keep away from worldly desires that wage war against the soul."

1 Peter 2:11

Today is the day to help the children of God to realize their self-worth. They don't realize they are worth more than gold. Every day, people are selling their souls to the devil at a cost they will never be able to pay back until they are made aware of their dark path and turn back to the light and find Jesus. I know because I too, for a very long time, had the evil one clutched onto me so tightly we were one. I couldn't tell the difference between the light and the dark. I really couldn't tell the difference between what was right for me and what was wrong. I am hoping my story will shed light for those who are caught up in his entrapment. May God help and have mercy on us all.

In our lives we all have pain. It gets accumulated over time and can weigh us down. We are like computers with a bunch of files that have never been deleted. The hurtful things people have said or done to us, and what we have said or done to others, get stored in our memory banks—not to mention all of our wounds from childhood when we didn't have much say or control over anything that happened to us. Can we ever heal from all of those years of negativity? For most people, it seems to just get buried. For me, it created shame and loneliness and an emptiness inside, a longing for something— but what? What is that thing that I longed for? To not feel bored with life and dispel that alone feeling?

It always seemed that I could never get enough; I always wanted more. Maybe it was making more money to have a boat or snowmobiles or a better house or that lake house or a bigger diamond on my finger. Mostly I worked all the time. Since I felt like such garbage inside, it made me feel so much better to accomplish things and be productive. I never felt as if I could accomplish enough. I never felt as if I had done enough. I kept striving for the approval of others through what I accomplished. I seemed to be an empty, bottomless pit. No matter what I put in to fill it, it was never full. I was a gerbil on the wheel in my cage. I looked out and I saw everyone else's life that seemed so much better than mine. Was it better? I kept on desiring more, and I never felt happy once I got it. What would it be like to be satisfied? What would it be like to be at peace? I thought it would be God's kingdom on Earth. Heaven.

I was searching for the ultimate love. I never felt satisfied with any relationship I had. I basically got stuck as a teenager and stayed that way for over twenty years, searching for love and obsessing about meeting my soul mate and getting married and having a family. That was my dream. That was what I wanted to do. There was a guy out there who was going to rescue me, like a knight in shining armor. These guys always looked so good to me at first. They always seemed amazing, and I would work hard to get them, doing whatever they wanted me to do. I just wanted their love, and to get it, I thought I had to be who they wanted me to be. I didn't know who I was, anyway. I thought I was easygoing and a go-with-the-flow girl. No demands and no voice. Until one day the resentment would build, and it would erupt like a volcano. It would all come spewing out—what I really thought of them. I think in a sick way I enjoyed it. I felt powerful. I felt strong. All the other times I felt so weak. I was so desperate to get a guy, but I never ended up liking him. This was repeated over and over and over again. I finally realized I was the common denominator in those relationships, and maybe I had to look at why I was attracting what I attracted. How could every man I attracted be selfish, cheap, and controlling? God puts people in our lives as mirrors, to show us things in ourselves that we don't want to see. My counselor once said, "Water seeks its own level." That statement still haunts me. I was an easygoing person without a voice. Well, that was my mask that I wore. That wasn't really who I was. The real me was buried under lots and lots of ego.

It didn't seem like anything was so wrong. Nobody noticed it as a problem. I was always waiting for a man—my soul mate—to rescue me. Christians only have one Savior, and his name is Jesus Christ. He died for me and you and everyone. For me, he was here for the day when my pain became unbearable. He was always here. It just depends on when we turn to him. How long does it take? How much pain do we have to inflict upon ourselves? When does that day come when we say, "I can't do this anymore"? At that point, it is either to take your own life—which I tried to do as a teenager, but more on that later—or maybe it is a slow death through an addiction that we deny having or are completely unaware of. This is what my story is about. I am a recovered sex addict. When you think of a sex addict, you probably think of pornography, voyeurism, incest, affairs, and sex with prostitutes—to name just a few. I know that's what I thought. You probably never thought it could be a girl looking for love through sex. I was a girl who had sex and love confused, who didn't have the word no in my vocabulary, who had never heard of the word hypersexual. A girl who never thought she was an addict. Even when I did realize it, most of my family and friends denied that I was one. If I was one, then what were they? My friend watched a movie on the Lifetime channel, called Love Sick: the Sue Silverman Story, about one woman's journey through sex addiction. She told me about that movie since we had opened up to each other about our pain and struggles. I bought that movie and watched it over and over again. It was before I knew I was a sex addict. I thought at the time I was only a love addict, but they are pretty close; it just sounded better to me at the time. In the movie, the girl was molested by her father. That wasn't part of my story. Nobody molested me as a child.

According the American Society of Addiction, the definition of addiction is the following:

Addiction is a primary, chronic disease of brain reward, motivation, memory, and related circuitry. Dysfunction in these circuits leads to characteristic biological, psychological, social, and spiritual manifestations. This is reflected in an individual pathologically pursuing reward and/or relief by substance use and other behaviors. Addiction is characterized by inability to consistently abstain, impairment in behavioral control, craving, diminished recognition of significant problems with one's behaviors and interpersonal relationships, and a dysfunctional emotional response. Like other chronic diseases, addiction often involves cycles of relapse and remission. Without treatment or engagement in recovery activities, addiction is progressive and can result in disability or premature death.

I grew up Catholic and was always a believer in God. I wore a cross around my neck for as long as I can remember. It was devoid of something, the cross I wore lacked our crucified Savior. I had to go on a journey through hell before I would call out to Jesus to help me. I had to break my soul and spirit before I would seek the Healer for repair. How did I even know to seek Jesus? I think it was that foundation of faith, that gift I had from my parents, of growing up Catholic and going to catechism and church for all those years so long ago. In the end, I had to surrender control of my life to Jesus. But I had to try everything else first. What I didn't see about myself was that I was a people pleaser, and I lacked a backbone. I didn't ever want anyone mad at me. I wasn't honest with anyone, most of all myself. I thought I had it all together. On paper it looked that way. I was educated and had a good job and was great with managing my money. I was just not good at managing my love life. I thought I just had bad luck. There was a whole lot more to it than that. I was forever seeking perfection in everything, yet I could never acquire it in my relationships. The pursuit of perfection without a relationship with Jesus is a downward spiral into hell.

I felt so much pain inside. When I would connect with a guy and get involved in a relationship, it would go away for a while. I would put the guy on a pedestal, which is where nobody should be. I was setting him up for failure. I only saw who I wanted to see. Until one day I couldn't hold up my rose-colored glasses. Then I suddenly saw him in this other light—this darkness of what a horrible person he was. It was one extreme or the other. It was how I saw myself too. Not a healthy way to live, to see yourself as awesome or as a piece of crap. I didn't even realize I was doing that. I mostly spent my life thinking I was ugly and worth less than other people, forever worried about what others thought. I asked three of my nieces what negative thoughts they had. They also worried about what others thought of them. That is the shame that binds us.

People with a lot of shame are candidates for addiction. The different vices used by the addict are ways to cope with our inability to meet everyone's expectations. We lose ourselves, who we are, and clarity of what we want. We engage in an impossible cycle of trying to meet and please everyone else's needs and wants and desires. We have trouble making decisions, and we feel we are unworthy of acceptance or belonging, not to mention love. So we become puppets. Our master is everyone else's opinion of us. We never feel quite right, as if there is something wrong with us, and we don't know what it is. We don't talk about it because we don't want anyone to know. If I had only known long ago that our self-worth doesn't come from what we do. It comes from whom we belong to: God. We are the beloved children of God. It only matters what He thinks of us. That is where I get my self-worth now. If only the entire world could comprehend this, especially the young people of the world.

We hide so much from ourselves. We all do it. There is not a person who doesn't. It's a constant, conscious surrender to God to keep the ego or false self from becoming who we are and taking over our authentic selves. It will always throw on a layer when you stop living mindfully, which is when you ignore how you are feeling, behaving, speaking and thinking. At first it is so hard to be mindful, to live in the moment. It is hard to ask why am I feeling a certain way or why do I spend my timing doing whatever it is that I do? It sounds so simple. It was the first thing my counselor had me do. That was when I realized I was numb. I never let myself feel, because that was so terribly painful for me. Why, though? Why had I lived my life for so long without realizing I was numb, unable to feel the full emotions of life? I had always thought of myself as an emotional person. I sure cried a lot in my twenties over being lonely and wanting a boyfriend, husband, and family. I got really excited a lot when I had something fun to look forward to, like a weekend in Chicago or Put-in-Bay with the girls. It seemed so ridiculous to me that my counselor would ask me questions to figure out how I felt about things that happened in my life that bothered me, and to most questions, I would reply, "I don't know." I think it was a hidden indication of why I had such a hard time making decisions. I felt I had to consult my dad and ask him what he thought. Our parents are wiser than we are, only because, with age, they've learned a few things the hard way. But it seemed I couldn't really think for myself all that much at times.

At one of my first few counseling sessions, I was given a list of adjectives as "homework." I had to practice becoming mindfully aware of how I felt and applying an adjective to that feeling. Even when I was in rehab, the word "mindful" was a huge topic. They had to teach us how to feel and to be aware of our feelings. I didn't want to feel, for what I felt was a mountain of shame. I felt I was a bad person and not deserving of love. I spent my life suffering from low self-esteem and trying to please everyone—all the while feeling guilty if I didn't do what someone else wanted me to do. It's a hard life trying to please everyone. I am thankful that I realized I only have to please one now: God. Once I learned that, everything fell into place. It was a long road with a lot of work to get to that realization and make it a part of my everyday life.

> "For God so loved the world, that He gave
> His only begotten son." (John 3:16)

Up until my marriage woes, I had my dad on a pedestal and thought my childhood was the most perfect childhood ever. But there is no such thing as perfect in anything except God. My parents both grew up very poor. They both came from alcoholic families among other addictions. Primarily the members of my dad's family were the gamblers, workaholics, and drinkers, and my mom's family were the eaters and drinkers—or at least that was how I saw them. There were no shopping addiction issues, as there was barely enough money, although nowadays with credit cards I am sure it wouldn't stop some people. Sometimes the family generational issues get passed on down the line. Although sometimes we see and learn who we don't want to be, my mom never went to the bar like her mom. My mom saw how the alcohol from the bar life had destroyed her family life. She didn't see an issue with my dad drinking every night since he didn't go to the bar. He was home with all of us. He worked long, hard hours at his automobile repair shop business. It seemed OK and normal to all of us for him to come home and have a few beers—"a few" being a six-pack, at least. We thought it was normal and that every dad did it. It was all we knew.

Until I was fifteen, my dad drank. Then suddenly he sold the business, and later he felt he had made a mistake in doing so. He blamed it on the drinking, and he quit. He started going to AA and realized how drinking had come first in his life. How we never went to a restaurant unless it served alcohol. How he drove us up north to our cabin with a six-pack of Michelob Light between his legs. During his twelve-step meetings, while listening to others' stories, he realized he had many stories himself of how drinking had created problems for him and his family. He told me a story of how he had thrown two bowling balls down the same alley and had gotten kicked out of the bowling alley, along with everyone he was with, and so the family left the bowling alley too.

At the time, I was fifteen and just starting my party days, so I didn't see it as a great accomplishment for him to quit drinking. There were no more cases of beer stacked up in the garage from my mom's stocking up on the stuff when it was on sale. Now my friends and I wouldn't be able to drink and put the empties back as if he had drunk them. So I thought it was kind of sad. Plus, my dad wasn't in his own world so much anymore. He was more in my life, which as a teenager is not what you want. I wasn't used to it. My dad selling the business and not working and not drinking anymore had suddenly turned my father into my very own micromanager. My father had realized he was a functioning alcoholic. At the time I didn't realize how that information could have helped me to identify my own addiction issues, if only I had been more educated about addiction and how it is passed on through the generations. My father never did go to a rehab center, and even though he believes in God and became a Catholic in the '60s, as far as I know, he doesn't have a relationship with Jesus. He quit drinking for ten years and drinks wine now instead of beer. He said, "Because it's healthy for you." My mom stays on him about how many glasses of wine he can have.

I had spent my life going from relationship to relationship. I was attracting the same person each time, but with a different face and body. At least I had the same experience with each of them each time. I was forever feeling used, controlled, whether overtly or covertly, and ignored. I was someone for their convenience, and I wasn't supposed to have hurt feelings or at least not acknowledge them. I was used to not having a voice. I grew up not being allowed to use mine. It was something I was good at, stuffing all of my emotions without ever realizing it. When you stuff, you will deal with the emotions at some point in some way. For me it was through masturbation or sex with a man, usually through a relationship—a man who was just as wounded as I was, a man who held many of the same traits as my father. Though, it wasn't my father's fault, not directly. My father is a wounded soul—wounded by his parents, who were wounded by their parents, each generation turning out to be wounded adults raising children with their own wounds from the childhoods we give them. Just as I have done to my son. We all do the best we can as parents. As someone profoundly stated to me, "The wounds I inflict on my children are a blind spot to me." Without seeking our Healer, Jesus, what chance do our children have?

I was at the park with my son, and there was a little boy playing with him for about a half hour. I don't have enough fingers and toes for how many times that little six-year-old said God's name in vain.

My son said to him, "By saying *God* in that way you are disrespecting Him."

The little boy said, "I don't care if I disrespect Him."

My son whispered to me, "Mama, he said he doesn't care if he disrespects God."

I told him that most of the world feels that way, and I realized later that I lived a long time that way too. I am so thankful to have come into union with my Savior. I have been remade new. He shone a light on my darkness. Without seeking Him, I never would have realized my sex addiction. I never would have tried to stop if I hadn't fallen in love with Jesus.

It seemed so normal and acceptable in our society to seek love and to have sex in every relationship I was in. What if your relationship never lasts, and the number of partners you have accumulates over time? You wake up and you are nearly forty, and you are still single and still alone. Then you take a closer look at your family, and you begin to see all of the functioning addicts spread out through the family tree. Each one with a different form of addiction, never bad enough to seek help. Yet each one is never satisfied with life and passes on the discontent to the next generation. My son has a different opportunity ahead. I know the darkness that lies within our family. I will be able to one day point it out, even if he chooses not to see it. One day it may help him to form a union sooner with Jesus than I did. Or maybe, just maybe, he will be one of the few who seek him on his own. I see girls at the pregnancy centers and women at my work and women with whom I have gone to college, all still struggling and still searching for that knight in shining armor. They don't know they need healing. A healing only Jesus can give. Everyone's path to Him is different. What will yours be? Will you do the work to find out?

Two

NEW GIRL IN TOWN

"Good indeed is the Lord, whose
love endures forever, whose faith-
fulness lasts through every age."

Psalm 100:5

At the age of fifteen, the summer before my sophomore year in high school, we moved up north to our lake house. Since my dad didn't like not working, he built a repair shop business. I enrolled in the local high school, which had a total of three hundred kids from seventh through twelfth grades. There were approximately forty-five kids in my class: thirty boys and fifteen girls. For some reason, there were a lot more boys up there than girls, or at least in my world. A few of the girls seemed to dislike me. I was a "city girl" to them—and competition. To the boys, I was exciting, a new girl. They could count how many times I said "like" and "you know" in a conversation with them. To them my parents were rich. Back home I was middle class. I was encouraged to try out for cheerleading, and I made it! I felt like a superstar. I was on the varsity football cheerleading squad since they didn't get enough girls for tryouts to have both varsity and junior varsity. Back home I couldn't make the dance team let alone try out for cheerleading. Competition was fierce back home with all the gymnastics involved. I had taken dance for ten years at a local studio, but just for fun. I never really gave it my all. So to be a cheerleader seemed awesome to me.

I thought things were looking up. I was in a new, small, country town, where I barely knew anyone, but I was going to be all right, or so I thought. The other cheerleaders were nice to me, and we had fun. I knew of other girls who didn't like me. One in particular wanted to beat me up. She told me her boyfriend liked me. I didn't even know who he was, even when she said his name. I was so well liked where I had moved from, with so many friends. That part was hard for me, really hard. To know there were people who didn't know me but already didn't like me was devastating.

I started to date a boy on the football team who lived near me and gave me rides to school; his name was Jerry. I clung to Jerry that first day of school. I will never forget the moment of walking through the doors of that high school with his cousin Gina, on our first day of school. I was so scared and nervous. I wanted to go back home where I had tons of friends and nobody wanted to beat me up.

Jerry was sixteen and in one grade above me. He was a junior, and I was a sophomore. He liked me and was nice to me. I liked him—other than the fact that he had really bad breath. I didn't look forward to kissing him. One fall Saturday night, I went to a wedding reception in town with him, and there was a city boy there. I was talking to him and being more talkative than I should have been. You could tell a difference between the city boys and the country boys, and I missed home and the superficial city boys, for that was what I was: superficial. Jerry and his friends noticed me liking the city boy. I heard his friend tell him, "I would drop her off on a dirt road somewhere, and let her find her way home." I couldn't find my way home at that time, even on a paved road in a car. When we were going home, he never talked, but I could tell he was mad. He drove really fast on a dirt road—and I was scared. When you drive fast on a dirt road, it almost feels like you are on ice or that the road is slippery. You kind of feel it in the tires against the dirt, like any minute you are going to spin out.

Jerry finally pulled over to the side of the road. It was very dark and desolate. We had sex. It was rough, and there were no words, and I just lay there. I felt like I was supposed to. He was my boyfriend. Why didn't I say no? Why didn't I say, "Hey, I can tell you are mad, take me home." Or, "Tell me why you are so mad? Is it because I talked to that city boy?" I just froze. I said nothing, and I did nothing. When he was done, he said I wasn't a virgin. That is who

I had my first sexual experience with. I gave myself away to a guy who didn't believe me that I was a virgin, a guy who used fear and anger as a manipulator. Why didn't I use my words to tell him how I felt? I just shut down. I was a girl who usually couldn't stop talking—but not when it came to confrontation.

I never had a voice that night. I don't even think I realized at the time how much it hurt, not just physically but emotionally too. I think I was already used to not having a voice. I was already used to not feeling pain. I was so used to shoving my sadness, anger and opinions down deep inside of me. I don't remember feeling anything except bad for talking to that city boy. From then on, we had sex for a while before he would take me home. He would pull over somewhere—and since it was a rural area, it was easy to find a place to pull over—and we would have sex. We didn't stay together long after that. I didn't like him. But it did start me on a path of self-destruction that I never could have imagined the effects of. It was the start of several short sexual relationships. I didn't learn until rehab that this experience was considered a rape. I said, "How? I never said no." They said I was set up by my parents not to. When I was raised, I was raised to be an obedient person. I was raised never to have an opinion or to show anger or sadness or much of any emotion except for a good attitude and a good time. I was never allowed to express how I was feeling. That would be considered "talking back," especially to my father. So for this moment in time, the psychologist said, "You were set up." I was not taught to say no or express how I felt. I kept everything in to the point that I couldn't even tell people how I felt about anything that I thought might make them mad or upset. I would shrug my shoulders and say "I don't know" or "I don't care." My girlfriend once told me, "I know when you don't agree with me; you look like a deer in the headlights."

My first sexual experience was considered a trauma. My counselor said most of my sexual experiences were probably a reenactment of that night on that dark dirt road. It's hard for me to see that, since I never said no. So many times in life we see only what we want to see. I am so thankful for all of my counselors who helped me to see and become aware of where my pain came from and why I had it and how to stop reenacting my trauma.

It wasn't long after that that I tried to commit suicide. It wasn't because of Jerry. I was really unhappy with living in the new town. When I was on the cheerleading squad, I was happy during football season. But then basketball season came, and they got more girls on the team, so they took me

from varsity to junior varsity, since I was a sophomore. Some girls at the school still didn't like me,
and it continued to bother me. I spent my entire life
just being who people wanted me to be so that they
would like me. When I messed that up, and I didn't
explain myself well enough to them to try to rectify
the situation, I would just beat myself up inside.

I found some valium one day while I was
cleaning, and one night I took them. There were
twenty-one of them, and I remember crying and
looking in the mirror and unwrapping each one and
looking at my face in the mirror, thinking how ugly
I was and how much I hated myself. I had so much
hate for myself, and I was so sad. My pain felt unbearable to me, and I wanted life to be over. I took
them. They were old and not as potent because of
that. It was like being drunk for three days from
what I can remember. Maybe it was two days, but
it felt like three. At the time I had my own phone
line because I tied up my parents' phone too much.
I had a boyfriend from about an hour away. I don't
remember, but I guess I called him or he called me.
He could tell something was wrong, or maybe I told
him. I don't remember. He called on my parents'
phone line and told them. My parents called all my
siblings to come home. I had three siblings, all married or with significant others and much older than

me. My sister who is ten years older than me, the one I was always closest to, stayed up all night talking to me to keep me awake. They were afraid that if I fell asleep I wouldn't wake up. I didn't remember anything the next day of what we had talked about. My parents told the cheerleading coach, and the coach told the girls on the squad, and they said I didn't really take the pills "because you would be dead."

My dad's good friend had a gay son who hung himself last year in the closet of his bedroom. People think people who commit suicide are selfish. They say they are selfish because of the pain they leave behind for everyone else, which is all true. Yet, people have no comprehension of the level of pain you are in when you do that to yourself. Recently my dad told me over breakfast what a bitch I was when I was a teenager for what I put them through. I agreed and said "I am sorry." (Under my breath, I said to myself, "I wanted to die back then. I was in pain.") Yet, I feel he has no compassion for the pain I was in. It is because he lacks compassion for himself. I really feel he is in pain. Maybe he doesn't know there is a way out. I think about the people I have known over the years who have died from suicide and the pain they must have been in. It makes me cry to know that Jesus could have healed them if they had known to want that healing from Him. But they didn't know. How do you convince people? How do you give people a desire in their hearts to fall in love with the one person who can save them from their pain? If we knew the answer, we would have less pain in the world.

I had a hard time making friends. I hung out with whoever would take me in. I hung out with the other wounded birds. The ones who drank, smoked pot, and smoked cigarettes. There was usually a party in the woods somewhere. My dad warned me that if I ever got caught drinking and driving, not to call him. One night I got pulled over with my boyfriend, Trey, and his friend in the car. We were at the only traffic light in town, and I saw the lights of the cop car behind me. I blew into a breathalyzer, and they wanted my dad's number. I begged them to take me to jail. I pleaded with them not to call my dad and to just take me to jail. It was a hot summer night, and they had big muscles and short-sleeve shirts on. I remember having my hands on their arms, pleading with them. I totally embarrassed my boyfriend in front of his friend, he later told me. They called my parents, and they came and got me. Trey's friend had his car at the gas station where we were, so he drove home.

After we dropped Trey off, I told my dad that I hated it where he moved me to, and that I drank, smoked pot and cigarettes, and now was having sex. I had been a straight-A goody-goody when I had moved up there. But I am sure that, in time, I would have done the same things back where I came from. It was the only time my dad pulled back his arm with his fist clenched, ready to hit me. I told him to go ahead and hit me, but my mom held his arm back and said, "Think about what you are about to do." Most of my life I felt she didn't protect me from him, but that time she sure did. They say we forget a lot of the bad and only remember the good times. The bad gets fragmented into different areas of our brains by our senses, such as smell, sight, touch, or sound. It doesn't all come together in a picture like the good times, so they are harder to remember. Maybe it's a blessing, but it makes it harder to put the pieces of our lives together.

When I was at rehab, I couldn't remember a whole lot of bad about my childhood. Just a couple instances, one being when I was a little girl playing poker with my mom, dad, and favorite aunt, Aunt Loretta, and her husband. I said something or did something wrong, and my dad raged at me and spanked me in front of everyone. I was so upset and humiliated. I remember another time around the age of five or six when my dad gave me little Loony Tunes character pins, but I did or said something, and he took them from me because I was bad. I don't remember much more than that. Isn't that weird? It's hard to make sense of how or why I became an addict. There is so much to addiction. It's like the Bermuda Triangle. Other than being yelled at and spanked, which is pretty normal for a kid, nothing bad happened to me, nothing that left anything I could see the physical effects of. Addicts think of themselves as bad people, and that comes from somewhere. The shame parents carry that doesn't get healed then gets passed on through the only style of parenting they know, which is how they were raised.

It seems that the wounds of childhood begin to come out when you are a teenager, or at least they did for me. When someone is drinking too much or doing drugs or going from relationship to relationship having casual sex, I see it as a big neon sign flashing, *Help me! Please help me!* I think most see it as a person who is selfish and a pain to everyone else. Addicts are selfish because they are in so much pain. When you are in that much pain, all you can do is think of yourself. It's really all you can do to keep yourself alive to cope with your pain. You don't know that at the time. You just think, "This is how I am; this is how life is." You don't know you are in a dark place in desperate need of healing and light. If someone would have told me at that time in my life that

I needed Jesus, I probably would have laughed at them. For me, I had to hit rock bottom. I didn't know there were nearly twenty years of destruction ahead.

Three

THE WOUNDED ATTRACT THE WOUNDED

"Be still before the Lord; wait for God."

Psalm 37:7

"This is how all will know that you are my disciples, if you have love for one another."

John 13:35

The first big party at the first weekend of college, I met a boy named Jay, and he grabbed my hand and took me around and introduced me to a bunch of upperclassmen who were his brother's friends. I didn't get it at the time, but Jay was gay. I was his cover. I went back to his room and we cuddled and that was it. He was the perfect gentlemen and walked me to my car. The night before, we had gone to Hardees to get food; we took my car since he had been drinking and I hadn't. He complimented my used, eight-year-old Oldsmobile and said how clean it was. The next day, I saw Jay in a brand-new Lexus—his dad owned several dealerships. I had no idea Jay came from a wealthy family; he was so down to earth and sweet. Jay continued to be friends with me but never pursued me romantically. The night he introduced me to everyone and held my hand, I thought he really liked me. He must have been worried or nervous about his brother's friends catching on to his being gay. I once asked him what his goal was in life, since his dad already owned twenty-five dealerships. He said it was to own fifty dealerships. Jay got through a four-year degree in a little over a year, June through August of the following year. I do believe there is some sort of connection between success and sex addiction, or maybe just addiction in general. Your excess of choice is your reward for working so hard. You just don't realize it's a chain, not a reward.

At the end of that first year of school I met another boy, Freddy, whom I dated off and on until just before Christmas of my senior year. He turned out to be gay too. I had suspected it by the summer before our senior year. He never wanted to have sex with me; he would only masturbate in front of me. He told me that he read it was supposed to be a turn-on for me; I didn't get it. I just thought maybe he thought I was gross or something. He didn't come out until after college. His dad had committed suicide when Freddy was thirteen and his brother was eighteen. I recently spoke to him about it, and he thinks it was because his dad knew he and his brother were gay. Another time he and his brother discussed that maybe his dad was gay and couldn't deal with the double life or charade anymore. Either way, that is a lot of pain to carry throughout life.

I was at a party at college, and this other girl we were talking to spoke of her father committing suicide. It was like the world stopped. She and Freddy spoke of how they felt about those dark days in their lives when they were so young. You could hear the pain in their voices. You could see the memories come up in their eyes of the pain, like they were experiencing it all over again. But they had someone, each other, who had experienced the same pain. You could see them bond over their tragic stories. The girl spoke of how she got on the school bus, not having a clue. Her sister had said to her, "Don't you think dad was acting strange?" She replied, "No." She was younger than her sister. She had so much regret for not understanding that her dad's good-bye to her that day would be his last. He knew what he was about to do. She said he did it in the shower, probably to avoid making a mess. Freddy's dad shot himself in the head in a rental car in Florida. Everyone has pain that we have no idea about. These tragic events that happen affect our behavior as we get older. We need to be sensitive to another's pain and be compassionate, and to do that, we first have to realize our own pain so we can heal and be compassionate with ourselves.

The summer before senior year, when Freddy found out his brother was gay, he was the best boyfriend. He tried so hard. He would leave notes on my car at work and surprise me to take me for ice cream—and he lived an hour away! One note he left on my car read, "Will a beautiful girl like you go for an ice cream? Come with me!" I thought "Wow, how sweet!" I looked up and there he was. It was the sweetest note anyone has ever written to me. He told me when we got out of school that he had something to tell me about his family. Once we visited his brother in Chicago that summer, I knew what it was. His brother was gay. I didn't press him for information, as I wasn't like that at the time. Now I would.

It wasn't long into the fall that he gave me a promise ring, but it was too late for me; the relationship was already over. I already thought he was possibly gay too. I started dating someone else before Christmas, and he took it hard. Later his friends teased me and blamed me for his being gay. Freddy and I spent most of our college years breaking up and getting back together. It was an addiction; I couldn't be away from him, but I wasn't happy when I was with him. I had never heard of love addiction back then, so I had no idea that was what it was. Our relationship wasn't healthy. Sometimes he called me when he was drinking and feeling sentimental. He joked about how we were supposed to have two kids and join the country club. He now has a partner he has been with for three years. He said, "That's twenty years in gay land!" He jokes about it, but I know he is in pain. He doesn't talk to the old gang from school that he was so close with. He says it doesn't bother him, but I can tell that it does. He medicates with alcohol and has been to rehab for drugs. He has a lot of pain.

I often think of Jay and Freddy and wonder—from what I know about addicts and the same level of water attracting the same level of water—did they have some form of sex addiction, a shade or degree of it? Could we be less critical and more sensitive and compassionate to look upon everyone as a wounded soul in need of healing? Would rehab help them hash through all of their wounds? I know for Freddy the rehab helped some, but he still sounds to me like he has a lot of pain. God is not in his equation for his continued healing. Rehab doesn't work for you unless you feel something is wrong and want to do something to change it. It is so hard to face truths about who we are and how we were raised and how that affects how we live our adult lives—not to mention the mental illness of addiction that generation after generation lives with and never does anything about unless it is severe. It's the family's "normal" dysfunctional heritage.

Is there some deep wound that people can't see or remember that makes them not like the opposite sex? Someone said that strippers don't even like men. It's why they are able to do what they do.

I feel they are empty as we all are without accepting God's love. I know Jesus didn't condone sinners, but He did heal them and help them. I know how painful it was being an addict and not knowing I was an addict. I know it was painful living the way I was living, yet I justified what I was doing. I knew premarital sex was wrong. I thought in this day and age Jesus couldn't possibly expect me to go without sex and masturbation, could He? I didn't know I was hypersexual and was in need of healing. I just thought, "This is the way I am, and I have to deal with it." I remember even thinking about how much fun it would be to be a stripper. That if my dad wouldn't have paid for my college, I would have done that to pay for it. I was such a cheap person and was extra-cautious about not getting into debt. I asked my counselor why I would think such a thing. He said, "You probably got a lot of negative attention and would like some positive attention." I watched a news report special on college kids—men and women both—who are strippers to pay for school. They probably have no clue of the darkness of addiction that lies beneath the objectification of their God-given bodies of the people they dance for and themselves

I think of when my son was at day care around the age of three, and his best friend, Bo, had two mommies, and he said he wanted two mommies. I thought maybe Bo's parents were divorced and he had a stepmom. I found out Bo's parents were lesbians. At the time, not understanding much about psychology, I didn't see any connection as to why out of all the kids in the class Bo and my son had hit it off the most. Later I spoke to Bo's mom about how I felt as an outsider being divorced, and she said, "Oh, you have no idea how my partner and I totally feel like that." I was carrying a lot of shame and embarrassment about my marriage not working out. The outcasts in society tend to cling to each other. Plus, you know how you like some people more than others. I felt like Bo's mom kind of had my personality of low self-esteem, being easygoing, not liking confrontation or anyone being mad at her, and having a hard time saying no. Her partner I never saw. I asked her if she had always been a lesbian, and she said no. She said that she thought it was more about meeting the right person. She went on to explain how her partner had been married and a teacher while she was a student in the class, and they met and fell in love.

About the time my son was five, Bo's mom came into my son's day care, pregnant with twins and Bo eventually left day care when they got a nanny to help while they were at work. Five years or more went by, and I ran into Bo's two mommies at a local restaurant with my mom. They were sitting up at the bar and something interesting happened. Now, being mindfully aware of how I feel at times, I noticed something. It was my first time meeting Bo's other mommy, and I was attracted to her. There was a spark between us. Not one that I would act on, but I could kind of get why the two of them ended up together. If God is not involved in your discernment, (discernment is seeking direction and understanding from God, if a decision you are making is of God, the flesh, the world or even the devil.), and you have not worked on healing your wounds and knowing what your wounds are, it's not the right person. It's someone you are hoping can ease your pain. Basically, discernment is trying to follow God's will and not yours, for the result that good will come from it.

Your wounds are like a beacon going off in you. Unaware of it yourself, your hurt is saying, "This one can heal your wounds." Yet, this one has the same negative traits your caregivers had from when you were a child. You try to heal yourself through this person. It's a disaster waiting to happen. Here in front of me sat two women, and my mom had no idea they were lesbians. I told her after we walked away. One was not manly and the other overly feminine. They were both quite feminine. But one gave out a spark as if ready to ignite dynamite just as the other men I attract can ignite a dangerously deadly spark.   I can be in a venue of three hundred people, and I will be attracted to people like Bo's second mommy, but usually in the male form. I am attracted to those wounds.

I had a sorority sister I hung out with who ended up coming out as a lesbian. My sister's close friend who was my brother's girlfriend for a short time came out eventually as a lesbian. My ex-husband's best friend growing up came out when he was in his early twenties. He said he knew since he was six. It was such a struggle for him to come out. They don't choose to have this life. They feel it is out of their control. Just as I felt my sexual wounds were out of my control. I didn't know I could be healed of it. I didn't know how hurt I was and in dire need of healing. If I would have had more hatred for men buried in me, then what would my life have been like?

There is a video called The Third Way about homosexuality and the Catholic Church, by Blackstone Films. There are four people in the video who share their stories of pain. They are gay and lesbian, they are Christians, and they are living chaste lives. It just melts my heart and makes me cry every time I watch it. We pass each other on the street and in the halls of work and school, never knowing each other's struggles. I could have used a lesson about empathy, just like most of us could. I didn't learn that I lacked it until rehab. I was told "it can be learned." Yes it can, and Jesus is a great teacher. In the summer of 2014, my son and I drove up to Thunder Bay, Ontario, to visit an amethyst dig site because he loves gems. We stayed at a hotel for a couple of nights in Thunder Bay. The first night there in the pool, my son was playing with a little girl. My son kept referring to her as "that boy" or "the boy over there." I asked the little girl her name, and she said that her name was Raya. She was wearing boys' board shorts and a swim shirt. I really didn't think anything of it, and I apologized to her mom for my son referring to her daughter as a boy. Her mom said, "Oh, it's OK. Raya has refused to wear girl clothes since the age of two; she wants to be a boy." Her hair had bangs and was cut to her chin. To me it was obvious she was a girl. I asked my son why he thought she was a boy. Was it just because of her clothes? He said, "No, he is a boy." I said, "No, she is a girl. Why are you still saying she is a boy?" I didn't understand, and I was trying to understand. We hung out with Raya for another three hours that night and the next evening as well for about three hours.

At one point, she gestured over to where her dad was. She told me about a time when she and her sisters had to walk a long way home from the school bus stop in the winter, and it was so cold and snowy.

She said her dad had the truck, and he had to go to court. She said, "Do you know what kind of people have to go to court?" I said, "No, what kind of people have to go to court?" She said, "Bad people have to go to court." I am not sure why she thought her dad was bad, but Raya had the look of sadness that I have never seen on a seven-year-old child. It was a deep and disturbing kind of sadness. On the second night of our pool evening at the hotel, Raya came out with a dress on, and her eyes were all red and swollen as if she had been crying something fierce. She told me she had a rash under her arms, so she wasn't going to swim anymore. Later she and my son tossed a football around, and I saw her run and jump and play, and she looked so happy. For the two nights we were there, that little girl didn't leave my side much when we were in the pool and by the pool. I think about her often. I pray for her journey ahead and know that no matter what all of that meant or didn't mean about her wanting to wear boy clothes and be a boy, she has a journey ahead in a life that can be unkind. How can someone at seven be so wounded? I wonder, does she have any foundation of faith at all to fall back on? What will her life be like? I have none of the answers to those questions. I send my love and God's love to her; somewhere there is a beautiful little girl who already hates being a girl. It's the last thing she said to me before saying good-bye. She said, "I hate being a girl." You know, I didn't think to ask her one simple question: why?

A lesbian, gay, bi, or transgender accepting oneself and coming out is a step toward the light. To stay hidden away in shame is to make the dark one happy. To love God more than anything, that takes conversion through God's grace, love, and healing. It is why He gave us His Son. Do you really think LGBT people are so different from those of us who aren't LGBT? There is no difference. We all hurt, we all need a Savior, we all have something that we do that we need saving from. It is perpetual, this saving that we need; the surrender is daily. We need saving from ourselves, from our wants that separate us from a union with the one who lives in us and created us, which is God. God's son, Jesus, is the way to mend the broken roads to get us there. Until we love and accept one another, even our wounds, and heal each other through God's love and mercy in Jesus's name, the enemy's work is at hand. Let one's brokenness take them to the Lord; don't be the reason for one's brokenness due to our lack of love and acceptance for them. Anything else is creating a barrier to the bridge they need to cross over to get there.

My brother's good friend Eddie has a twin brother who is gay but who won't accept he is gay so he drinks to deal with it. He has acted out on it over the years, but he won't come out. He is not OK with it. How is he ever supposed to heal from it if he won't accept it? He is in denial just like I was about my addiction. Eddie thinks the drinking is a separate issue from his brother being gay, but addiction is addiction. The world just doesn't understand what sex addiction is. Eddie and I used to make out like the world was going to end even though he is nearly fifteen years older than me. When I was a teenager, sometimes on the weekends my parents would send me to my sister's, and if she and my brother both had something going, they would have Eddie hang out with me. We never had sex because I was sixteen, and I later found out he did have sex with others that I was close to. It's so odd to me, yet it makes sense, this spider web that sex addiction weaves. It's like an underground connection of tunnels in the dark.

In counseling they said I had an attachment issue that stemmed from not attaching to a caregiver in the early years of life. If your caregivers are unable to attach to you emotionally, you can spend all the time in the world with them and it won't help you. The issue is often handed down. It's part of the root of the addiction. The chain has to be broken. Attachment issues are part of the high divorce rate statistics and a big part of the sex addiction explosion. We have superficial connections (unable to give and receive real love), are unable to trust, are controlling, and have a fear of intimacy (the real kind), among other things. It all falls under the category of narcissism. It explains our world. It's like the evil serpent planted a bomb years ago, and we are just now feeling the effects of it or seeing the picture come to light.

I think of all the love I thought I was giving as well as so many hugs and kisses to my son. Looking back, I wasn't mentally or emotionally healthy. So what have I done? How severe is the damage? I won't know until he is older. People spend so much effort on discipline from ages five to eighteen. It's the emotional destruction we do to our children from birth to age five, due to our lack of knowledge about our mental health state, which needs to be addressed. If people continue to have an issue with attachment and don't receive healing for it, we will continue to destruct ourselves in our sick society. Individually, we are a mirror of how sick our society is as a whole. It explains why the family is dying. I am healthier now, and I will love my son regardless of who or what he grows up to be. I will pray for him and never give up on his conversion, just as Saint Monica did for her son, who also became a saint: Saint Augustine. God have mercy on our world. Please guide us to heal our world.

My behavior for most of my life acted out in a way as if there was a natural tendency and compelling force. It is so hard to accept our destructive behavior as anything other than normal because we naturally try to hide our pain. To encourage suppression is to make the evil one smile with delight. For nothing grows in the dark except mold. We need light to grow and to go through a conversion. Jesus can heal if you seek Him with your heart, mind, body, and soul, but you have to want it. There are people at the bar who need help or people in the casino who need help or people who are way overweight who all need help with why they seek what they do to feel better, even though it is hurting them. A few of my cousins have had gastric bypass surgery, only to gain the weight back. They probably never thought of rehab for their eating instead. Plus, they don't know that God can help. The first step of the twelve-step program is to surrender to your higher power. Your higher power is your answer to everything. Are you ready to hear it and respond?

I was a huge sinner. Now I am in love with the Lord. I have peace and joy and want nothing. Jesus is for real. God is here. I remember being twenty-eight and begging for His help. So what took me almost another ten years? I went through hell on Earth. How much hell do you have to go through on Earth before you will surrender and ask for his help? Once you are in union with Jesus, you no longer fear death. For a reason, you have a place to go. You know where you are going. I tell you this because I know the pain I was in and know there are so many others hurting, and your behavior and actions and choices are proof. You can be healed. Your life can be better. What took me so long? I don't have that answer for sure. I think the words control and surrender pretty much sum it up. I wanted to be in control and wasn't ready to surrender my life to God to be in control. He is always in control of our lives. I just fought Him for it. The blessings don't come until you surrender to Him.

Four

SHACKING UP

"Be sober and vigilant. Your opponent the devil is prowling around like a roaring lion looking for someone to devour."

1 Peter 5:8

When I met my ex-fiancé, I saw him as my knight in shining armor. I was no longer lonely or sad. I was in love, or so I thought. They never lasted long, those feelings. People can only keep up the charade for so long. He and I each comprised the negative traits from our childhood caregivers, our parents. He probably felt all-consumed by me, and suffocated. I felt he was the controlling father that I couldn't get away from, always there telling me what I was doing wrong, and what I needed to be doing. I forever was a teenager rebelling. His name was Craig, and he was from out of state. I had met him shortly after Thanksgiving of my senior year of college. His family was a lot like mine. His mom was a stay-at-home mom like mine, and his dad owned a business. The men were waited on in his family like my dad was, because he worked so much. Craig proposed to me over the summer, and my future sister-in-law's brother said I looked like a scared little girl. I think I knew deep inside that I didn't want to marry him, but I said "yes" anyway.

Just before Valentine's Day of that following year before my twenty-third birthday, his dad had my job transferred. His father's business had dealings with the company I worked for. I heard my boss inside his office, yelling, "What am I, chopped liver?" I was in a manager-in-training job through him, a position that he had created and was testing out on me. I messed up his plans, leaving in the middle of my year of training.

A few short weeks later, Craig moved me out of my tiny apartment and into his house. It didn't take long to see that he didn't treat me the way he did when we were at school. He expected a nice dinner when he got home—not macaroni and cheese and salad out of a bag. I didn't know how to cook. At school, he cooked, or he took me out to dinner. His parents had cut off his credit card that they had been paying for, and he wanted to settle into domestic life. I got a glimpse of what marriage would be like with him, and I didn't like it. There was a pattern building with the men I attracted in that I just wasn't seeing at the time. At school there were signs from him that this was how life would be, but I chose to ignore them. Once, we got in a fight at school and I walked away from him, and he snapped his fingers and said, "Get over here," and I said, "I am not your dog." That was a huge red flag and a precursor of how our engaged life of living together would be.

One night while we were watching television, he brought his fist toward me as if he would strike me and then stopped an inch from my face, and I jumped. He said, "Just wanted to make sure you were still scared of me." It was a few months after that when I told him I wanted to move back home since I was not happy. He said, "You have a life better than any one of your friends." He was speaking about money. I had a used truck from the dealership that I didn't get to pick out and that I didn't like, which I drove for free. I would have rather had my ten-year-old Oldsmobile. I had a cell phone before almost anyone had a cell phone, and that was also paid for through the dealership. Most of that money that I earned by working went into my savings or was used for shopping money. Yet I wasn't happy. My father didn't teach me to marry for money. My father told me often, "Money can be the root of all evil." I am thankful for that. It helped me to make my decision to leave, even though my brother and dad both said, "Are you sure you want to leave? Craig's family does a lot of really cool stuff." The straw that broke the camel's back was when Craig told me that if I tried to leave, he would soak me in sulfuric acid, cut my jaw plate out with a chainsaw, and bury my bones behind the dealership. Maybe he was just joking in a serious tone, but I was not going to stick around to find out. Who even thinks—let alone says—something like that?

When I knew Craig was going on a business trip, my dad hired a moving truck to move my things, and I booked a flight back home. I left my engagement ring in a card and wrote that I was sorry it had to end this way. I was scared. I was scared that I would never be able to leave if he was home and knew about it, and if I tried, what would he do to me? I had gotten so depressed trying to decide and planning all of this. I would come home from work and just get in bed and sleep. It was the severest my depression had ever been and ever was in my life, aside from when I tried to take my own life as a teenager. Craig represented my hopes and dreams of falling in love and getting married and having a family. It was a fantasy. I could see myself ten years down the road, married and miserable, with two kids tied to me, and me cooking spaghetti sauce and never getting back home to visit my family. I felt unwelcome there and that his family hated me.

I could have sold my soul to the devil and married him. I could have never worked and just shopped, with nice cars and a big house and lots of stuff. His family had a cabin with snowmobiles, a condo in Florida, and a house on Lake George that they rented every summer. It was the most beautiful lake I had ever been to, surrounded by God's glorious sights of nature and mountains, yet I couldn't do it. That day in August, I said good-bye to the lake, knowing I was leaving three days later. It was the day I said good-bye to Craig and his family but from the inside. I know I hurt him and his family, and they thought I was terrible and didn't understand. My heart broke that day. A part of my dream had died. The fantasy was over, and reality was ahead. As I was outside with the movers, the neighbor lady stuck her head out her window and asked what was going on. I said, "I am leaving because my fiancé is controlling."

Her reply was, "If he is controlling now, he will be worse when you are married." Looking back, that was my confirmation, my "God wink," that I was doing the right thing. At the time, I didn't think too much about God, so I just smoked cigarettes that day, talked on the phone to my girlfriend in Florida, and paced the floor asking her if I was doing the right thing. I never thought to ask God. If I would have, I wouldn't have needed all those cigarettes.

The reality of moving back home and seeing all of my college friends three weeks later, as I stood as maid of honor in my best friend's wedding from college, flooded me like a tsunami. Freddy would be there, and I had ended things with him to be with

Craig. Freddy had banned me from his fraternity parties, and when I had left school, it was not on a good note with him or his friends. My best friend was marrying his good friend. I went to the wedding with not an ounce of self-esteem. That shame was nothing new to me; I just felt it more at that time. Looking back, the depression and anxiety I was in were covered by a fake smile and a lot of drinking that weekend. Freddy was there and shockingly he was nice to me. We went dancing at a gay bar after the wedding, near the hotel everyone was staying at. We never could out dance each other. After a while we went back to where everyone was partying in the hotel room, and he painted my toenails in front of everyone, and I could tell by their looks that they thought it was weird. I thought it was fun.

Also, I had my five-year reunion from high school that fall. I had no car and no job, and I was living with my parents, two and a half hours away from the big city for interviews and where my friends were working. I felt like a failure. I was used to that; that is the wardrobe of the addict. All the while I was unaware of my addiction and how it would grow in the years ahead.

I gave to men everything I had, hoping they would love me, really love me. I lived that way, justifying everything due to the pain I was dealing with and the sickness that I had, though I had no idea of its presence. It is an accepted sickness in society. In fact, I look more normal in society being a sex addict than I do having a relationship with Jesus. I spoke of sex and joked of sex, and sex was always on my brain. I would talk about a good-looking guy I saw or explain the "perfect" guy as someone who made a lot of money, was well educated and from a good family, liked to work out, and was nice looking. That didn't work out so well for me with Craig. Of course, I was superficial, objectifying men just as they were objectifying me.

Craig once asked me, "Why does your stomach stick out like that?" I was a size four at the time. Maybe it was just my posture, due to my low self-esteem. That comment didn't help the belief that I already had of not being skinny enough. I had a distorted body image. Craig was a size thirty-eight waist at the time of that comment, he wasn't exactly thin himself. I hear many times men complain of their spouse or girlfriend's figure, all the while supporting nothing close to a trim and fit figure, an obvious case of double standards. They have no idea how cruel it is to think or even say that about the one they supposedly love. But I think women compete with other women regarding their figures, even more than they care what men think.

I ate tuna fish for lunch nearly every day at work for about five years because I heard someone lost a lot of weight by doing that. After that it was chicken and spinach every day at work for lunch and something equally healthy for dinner nearly every night during the week. I really could identify with the Karen Carpenter story, but I never took it as far as she did. At rehab they asked me if I counted calories, and I said, "No." Looking back, that was a lie. What do you call the way I ate? I didn't count the calories, but I knew what was not high in calories and ate that. I was told that many women sex addicts suffer from some degree of anorexia or bulimia. We are consumed by our bodies and what they look like; we objectify them. I just thought I was normal since I was forever comparing myself to the girls in the Victoria's Secret catalogs. I remember thinking I hit the jackpot when they came out with a bra that made your breasts look two sizes bigger. It's so cool to not care about that stuff anymore. I pondered getting a boob job for years. I always wanted big boobs, but not anymore. I'm so happy I didn't go through with that idea. God thinks I am beautiful just the way I am, so now I finally feel beautiful inside and out, and I think it shows by the light in my eyes.

It took me so long to get over my relationship with Craig—nearly six years. I cried over him, but I was crying over the fantasy of our relationship, not our actual relationship. Less than three months after I left, I found out Craig had gotten a girl pregnant, but it was an ectopic pregnancy. They were going to get married until they found that out. He was married to someone else not long after that. I was devastated. I couldn't even think of dating, let alone having sex with someone else at the time, but not for long. Pia Mellody's book, Facing Love Addiction, was very helpful to me. Love addiction is described in a few different ways. It could be someone pining away for someone for twenty-five years. Or it is often during a marriage or relationship when one person isn't into the other and dives into work or has an affair, and then the spouse will feel ignored or neglected and do something similar, which causes the other spouse to reengage. It is a game of back-and-forth, with neither party being on the same page at the same time. It makes for an unhealthy relationship and explains many of the affairs that go on so easily with people meeting at work, through Facebook, or on dating websites like Adult Friend Finder, or worse, through the Ashley Madison website that states, "Life is short, have an affair," with a picture of a wedding ring.

I know people close to me who have slept with more people while being married than before they got married. I beg them to go to confession and seek healing for their past. I have friends who have told me they have had sex with many more people than I have, and they are now married and have been for ten years or more. I often wonder what their marriages are like. Sex and love addiction don't just go away. My girlfriend told me her husband worries during the day about whether they are going to have sex that night. He is a big fan of anal sex, and she told me, "Dawn, it never feels good."

What I went through after I left Craig, even though it was my choice, was withdrawal. I medicated by increasing my partners during that time. Looking back, it was the most destructive time in my life. The relationship hopping increased. It took me until I got pregnant to sober up a bit from my unknown sexual addiction. According to Psych-Guides.com, the Departmental Management of the USDA states that "pregnancy is a common side effect that can occur due to risky behavior. In one survey, nearly 70 percent of women with sex addictions reported they'd experienced at least one unwanted pregnancy as a result of their addiction."

The way I lived is acceptable for today's culture. Therefore, why would I think there was anything wrong with me? How I lived for over twenty years can be seen on most television shows. The one-night stands and broken relationships, with everyone looking for love and the perfect mate with the best body, and without much awareness of the source of enormous pain and scarring from broken relationships.

I think of my friend Jean who had a ten-year affair with a man from her work. He always had an excuse to explain why he wouldn't divorce his wife. All her friends tried to tell her that if he didn't do it now, he never would. Jean waited and took trips up north with him and ate out in restaurants with him, and he would come over on Saturday mornings, telling his wife he was going to work. He bought Jean lots of gifts, but I think it came down to the fact that he didn't want to give his wife half of what he owned. His lust for money was greater than his lust for my friend. Jean is ten years older than I am, and she's still single. She has two daughters in their twenties now, and I wonder what their lives will turn out like. I will never know the skeletons in their closet like I do their mom's. Will the way their mom lived her life affect them? I guarantee it.

I heard of that man having sex with a few other girls from work, too. He is so successful at work. He stands out as a leader and a driver of change and improvement, and nobody would ever know. The drive for money, power, and control has an even darker, more twisted side than anyone will ever realize, even as they pass that guy in the hallway. Sadly I have many, many other stories such as this. They all end the same way. *How we live our lives on earth determines where our immortal souls will spend eternity.* Sex addiction is ruining so many souls, their earthly human lives *and* their souls for the next world. Many people don't care enough to think about it. Being oblivious to it is bliss for them. I think they just don't know, like I didn't know. But in time it can break a soul.

I had the gift of being with my friend Sonya as she took her last breath, but what I saw in the last minutes of her life haunts me. She opened her eyes and her mouth wide and appeared to scream, but nothing came out. I am unable to erase from my memory the look of terror that was in her eyes, even though I want to. She then pushed away with her palm, out into the air, and nearly moved her entire body as if trying to get away from something or someone. Lastly, she closed her eyes with a frown upon her face as if she were beginning to cry—and then she was gone. I went to her side, and what I saw in the corner of her eye was one tiny tear not big enough to slide down her face. I touched it with the tip of my finger and held that tear on my finger, just staring at it. That all happened so fast I didn't know what it was. I still don't. It did disturb me, though, to the core.

I had gotten an e mail a few weeks earlier from a man in the Christian network group I was part of at work. He was a volunteer through Grace Hospice, which was, as he stated, "a strong Christian organization that comforts those who are dying." He wrote down some things he learned in training and the different things that some people may experience shortly before they die, along with an explanation as to why. He felt it was time to share it with everyone who was on the e mail distribution list. Another coworker told me how that e mail had disturbed her. I told her, "The closer you get to the Lord, the less it will bother you. Keep seeking him." As I had already had my encounter with Jesus, accepted His love and started my relationship with the Lord at that point, what happens after we die no longer scared me, as I felt peace about getting to go home. I got that e mail out and one of the five items he listed matched closely to what Sonya experienced.

There is not a day that goes by that I don't think about my friend. I live each day differently, with more courage to speak God's truth, for I am in "God's family business of saving souls," as Father Patrick stated it. We all can be intentional disciples and part of God's family business. I spoke to Father Marko about what happened to my friend, and he said, "God wants my salvation even more than my mother does. His love for me is even more than my mother."

I can't help but wonder if Sonya had a relationship with Jesus. Did she accept Him as her Lord and Savior? Did she have sorrow in her heart for her sins and surrender to Him? Did she believe in God? I thought she believed. There was evidence of things in her home: a cross and scripture that hung on the walls. She wore a cross around her neck, and she was baptized in her mid-thirties. I think about the healing that Jesus gave her. She had cancer and had an operation to remove what was left of the cancer that was indicated from the scan. When they opened her up, the cancer was gone. She had not had any more treatment since the scan. The doctor called it a phenomenon, not a miracle. Sometime later, Sonya called me to tell me her grandmother had healed her. My heart sank. I didn't have the courage to tell her, "No, Jesus healed you. Give the credit to him." Her grandmother could have interceded for her, but ultimately Jesus is the only one who can heal. Maybe that is what she meant?

First of all, then, I ask that supplications, prayers, petitions, and thanksgivings be offered for everyone, for kings and for all in authority, that we may lead a quiet and tranquil life in all devotion and dignity. This is good and pleasing to God our Savior, who wills everyone to be saved and to come to knowledge of this truth. For there is one God. There is also one mediator between God and the human race, Christ Jesus, himself human, who gave himself as ransom for all. (1 Timothy 2:1-6)

In time her cancer came back, and I kept thinking I had more time with her. I was in denial, I suppose, for the doctors had told us she didn't have much time left. I thought I had more time to talk to her about her relationship with Jesus. The truth is that I was a coward. I have to live with myself, and I realize now that God doesn't want me to blame myself, even though it's hard not to. He put others besides just me in her path to bring Jesus to her. A family saw her in a parking lot of a department store sitting, in the passenger seat of a car, waiting for someone. Her scarf was on her head, and they could tell she was more than likely going through treatment for cancer. They knocked on her window and asked to pray over her, and she let them. She told me about it. She said, "Dawn, they were like you; they prayed over me the way you do." I realize now why it's hard to be a Christian, as I have heard people say. My life was extremely hard as an addict, but this is a different type of hard because it's not about me. It's hard because it's about everyone else's eternal life. I get a second chance in every person that I encounter; I listen for the Holy Spirit to prompt me to be Jesus's hands, feet, and mouth, and through Christ Jesus I have the courage to do so.

Sonya went to mediums and believed that the medium could receive messages from her grandmother. At the time, I didn't know the Bible well, the scripture and God's word and how God views mediums. As Saint Jerome said, "Ignorance of scripture is ignorance of Christ." Sonya was a strong personality and believed that you just have to be a good person. Everyone at her funeral said she was a good person. So many people said she was in heaven and in a better place. I just was not sure if she was or was not, but I couldn't tell anyone what I had seen. I had to keep it to myself. She was so young. Everyone was having such a hard time with her death as it was. I tried to tell someone close to me. I told my other friend that I saw something bad, and she said, "Dawn, I don't want to know. I never want to know."

When someone dies, we all assume everyone goes to heaven. It's more lies from the evil guy that justifies how we can live a life without a relationship with Jesus; however, we want and expect that Jesus is going to hook us up with heaven at the last moment of our lives, which He may for some—only He knows our hearts. It's a huge risk to wait. Why wait? God tried to reach me for so long. I am so thankful that I finally took His hand. I pray for my friend's soul. When I have told a few people about my friend's last breath, it scares some of them, and others say maybe she just didn't want to die. She didn't want to die. She was very young. Yet, I think it was more than that. I will never give up hope and prayers for God's mercy on her soul. For I don't know where she is; maybe she is in heaven or purgatory. I think of her as being in one of those places, as it's the only way I can get out of bed every morning. I assume that is why everyone thinks that way for everyone they know who has died. Yet, it gives us no reason to live a different life, a life in union with God's only son. As Father Riccardo has said, "We have to know God's law to know how to live." Please, God, have mercy on our souls.

I wish we didn't have free will, but we do. God can't make us love Him. We have to want to fall in love with Him and accept His love and seek Him so that he will seek us. We have to be pure and holy and ready to face Him at all times. The parable of the ten virgins is enough to keep me ready:

Then the kingdom of heaven will be like ten virgins who took their lamps and went out to meet the bridegroom. Five of them were foolish and five were wise. The foolish ones, when taking their lamps, brought no oil with them, but the wise brought flasks of oil with their lamps. Since the bridegroom was long delayed, they all became drowsy and fell asleep. At midnight, there was a cry, "Behold, the bridegroom! Come out to meet him!" Then all those virgins got up and trimmed their lamps. The foolish ones said to the wise, "Give us some of your oil, for our lamps are going out." But the wise ones replied, "No, for there may not be enough for us and you. Go instead to the merchants and buy some for yourselves." While they went off to buy it, the bridegroom came and those who were ready went into the wedding feast with him. Then the door was locked. Afterward the other virgins came and said, "Lord, Lord, open the door for us!" But he said in reply, "Amen, I say to you, I do not know you." Therefore, stay awake, for you know neither the day nor the hour. (Matthew 25:1–13)

Five

BABIES

"Children are a gift from the Lord,
the fruit of the womb a reward."

Psalm 127:3

I remember Suzy, the girl I took in high school to have an abortion, and what a horrible experience that was for her—and for me too. I remember all of the people in the waiting room, crying and being there for four hours. It was such a long process, and when you are sixteen years old, it seems longer than the actual four hours we were there. I will never forget the two girls who had driven down to Saginaw from Mackinaw. They told the girl that either she wasn't really pregnant or they didn't get all of the baby's parts, so she had to come back. She was hysterical. I remember her friend taking her out of there, and they were huddled together with their arms around each other. Young girls were there with their boyfriends and so sad. Moms were there with daughters. I don't know what people think it is like at those places, but it definitely is not an easy decision for these girls, or at least it didn't used to be. Until we can reach out to girls for healing before they get pregnant and make them aware of love and sex addiction, abortion will be the norm as part of our sick society.

I remember my other friend Adel who screamed at her boyfriend from across the room at a party, "I'm pregnant, you &%$#!"

Then he said, "We will just get it taken care of." That's what they had done the last time she was pregnant.

She yelled, "I knew you would say that! I am five months pregnant, so it's too late!"

Talk about seeing some serious pain. I didn't even go to her and comfort her. I was shocked. I didn't know what to say. What she must have been feeling and going through—I wasn't there for her. I just stood there. I am so sorry for that. That couple is still together today. Their daughter is in her mid twenties now.

Then there was my friend from college, Olivia. She was getting married in the fall and found out she was pregnant early in the spring. Her fiancé didn't want her to be pregnant at their wedding, as most of his family talked badly about his brother who had gotten his girlfriend pregnant before they were married. She was also worried because she had family coming from far away and arrangements had been made for flights, and she didn't want to walk down the aisle six months pregnant and disappoint everyone. She said she was leaving it up to her fiancé to decide.

I told her not to have an abortion. "You always wanted to be a mom. You love children; you were a nanny during college and loved it," I told her. I knew from Suzy's and Adel's experiences that Olivia would regret it.

She looked beautiful in her size six wedding dress. Beauty hides pain.

We didn't speak much after her wedding. I don't know why, but we aren't close friends now. I missed her so much over the years. I wonder if I had a love addiction with her too. I read that you can have it with friends and even children. Not the sexual part but the addiction part of it. Ironically, after fifteen years of not seeing her, I ran into Olivia at a department store. We hugged; it was great to see her. Suddenly two of her three children came walking up. Amazingly for this day and age, she is married to the same man. All I could think was that there is supposed to be a fourth child. I wanted to say, "You have a sibling in heaven with little angel wings on her or him. Jesus and the Blessed Virgin Mary are all watching over that child until you and your parents get to heaven."

I think of all the factors that go into abortion. I understand why Jesus hated hypocrites so much. He knows our pain and why we do what we do. That is why He is so merciful. The rest of us don't know another's pain, do we? Yet we judge and we judge. Let's let God be God. If we could love more, each of us, and judge less, think of how our world would change. I think of how upset that family would be if they knew that their condemning words on Olivia's sister-in-law who got pregnant out of wedlock were a deciding factor in the killing of a baby in the family Two of the three girls I knew who had abortions were my best friends at the time of their abortions. All three got pregnant again within six to nine months after their abortions. I feel they were replacing the babies they had lost and suffering from Post Abortion Stress Syndrome.

Two of the three were not married when they got pregnant the second time. All of them had one thing in common—that it was never discussed again. I mean, what do you say? I remember being sad for them. I don't remember it disturbing me as much as it does now. Not until I was faced with my own unplanned pregnancy did it leave an impact on me, which would be a huge factor in my own baby's fate.

I ran into Suzy after about twenty years of not seeing her. Now I was able to speak with Suzy. I asked her if we could go to lunch. I brought up the abortion that I took her to have, and we spoke of how painful it was for her.

She said, "There was a void afterward, a loss, a death."

I asked her if her second pregnancy was on purpose.

She said, "It was with whoever bought the alcohol that night, and they didn't use any protection."

She married that man, and they had another child together and then divorced. Suzy has since remarried and has two more children who are now teenagers. The children from her first marriage are now in their early twenties. She is the grandmother of a beautiful little girl. The parents of that little girl were never married and are no longer together. I wonder if Suzy's granddaughter will repeat the family pattern of pregnancy outside of marriage. I pray for her to have a different experience in her life.

I asked Suzy how she feels about abortion now. She said I opened a wound, but she would not have wanted to have that baby because of who the father was and who she would have been tied to. I can relate to that. Yet, if I had not kept my baby and not married my son's father, even though it was a painful marriage, I might never have learned everything I have about myself and who I am. I am thankful to my son and his father. It sent me down another road, one with light at the end. Suzy let me pray over her before we parted ways. I asked for the Lord to heal her and bring her into His light.

I asked Suzy, since she has teenagers, what she knew of abortion now compared to how it was when she had one back in 1990. She said back when she had one it was shameful. Now it is more acceptable, and the girls are using it as birth control, having more than one abortion in some cases. Thank God for Rachel's Vineyard. Rachel's Vineyard is a healing weekend retreat for the mind, body, and soul for those who have experienced or been a part of an abortion. It is a powerful way to experience God's merciful forgiveness, healing, and love. We have a lot of hurting and wounded souls out in the world from this. Too many people don't know that children are a gift from God, an amazing miracle. The children are the ones who are hurt the most and are the victims of sex addiction. They are sucked out and tossed out with the trash. The parents suffer the consequences by way of regret. It's a hidden shame. Most don't ever bring it up. It is never to be talked about again. It's what the evil serpent likes, for us to keep things hidden in the dark closet of our souls. Light heals—bringing things out into the light, God's light. I have many others in my life who have experienced the pain and sin of abortion. Nobody discusses their abortions. They are usually not brought up again. How many teenagers out there don't know their parents had an abortion? How many people will repeat the family tradition? How many parents won't know of the grandchildren who were murdered before they even left the womb?

I volunteer at the pregnancy center in my town. The only difference between most of those girls and me is that I didn't have a learning disability and/or my dad paid for and insisted that I go to college. Most of the girls seem to bounce from their baby's daddy to a different boyfriend and sometimes back to their baby's daddy, all in a matter of less than three years. I only have some of the girls as my clients for half that long. There are a ton of pamphlets at the center, covering subjects ranging from venereal diseases to parenting to healthy food choices. Yet, there is nothing on love and sex addiction. This world is unaware that the evil-eyed snake is destroying the family, and therefore our world, through these addictions. Most differ in their shades and degrees of it, but all are lonely and empty, on a dark path leading to no good place.

Love is patient, love is kind. It is not jealous, love is not pompous, it is not inflated. It is not rude, it does not seek its own interests, it is not quick tempered, it does not brood over injury, it does not rejoice over wrongdoing but rejoices with the truth. It bears all things, believes all things, hopes all things, endures all things. (1 Corinthians 13:4–7)

From the age of sixteen to twenty-nine, I was on the pill. I had irregular periods, and the doctor said birth control pills would regulate them. Why it was so important to know when my period would start, instead of just letting my body tell me the signs is beyond me. My sister worked for a gynecologist, so she got my birth control pills for free for most of those years. I had premarital sex from age fifteen until just before my thirty-seventh birthday. Birth control makes it very convenient for sex addicts not to have to stop to think about what they are doing. What I once viewed as my saving grace contributed to the evil one at work, nearly getting my soul for all eternity.

Yet, I sporadically called upon God for help. I prayed my bedtime prayers most nights and went to church for most of the big holidays like Easter and Christmas. I knew God didn't want me to have premarital sex, but I justified it for the culture we lived in. I justified it as "He must accept it due to the culture of the day and age." I used to pray to him, "Please, Lord, help me wait six months to have sex when I am dating." Sex was such a strong force in my life. The sexual wounds that I didn't realize I had led me to think that surely God didn't expect me to wait until I would marry someone. He must understand. I never thought of it as a barrier to my drawing closer to Him. The devil's lies don't appear as lies at all. In a way, his lies allow us to live without much awareness of the real source of our pain. I really thought a man would save me and take away all my problems and pain. I really felt that I had to keep trying and keep searching for this man who would rescue me.

At the age of twenty-nine, I got pregnant. My boyfriend George and I had broken up in April after his behavior on our vacation to Jamaica. From that time on until July, George pursued me with calls and flowers and cards left on my porch. In June, I was supposed to have my gynecological appointment, but there was a sudden death in my doctor's family so my appointment was canceled. I couldn't reschedule until the beginning of August. My supply of birth control pills had run out, and my prescription had expired. I could have called to get more pills, but I think I figured since I wasn't dating anyone I would be fine. George was still calling me now and then. He caught me in a weak moment, which I'm sure is what he was hoping for, a couple of weeks into July and asked if I wanted to go to dinner. He came over, and we had sex, because if a guy took me to dinner, I felt like I was supposed to do that. Plus, he was my ex-boyfriend, and we used to have sex, so what did it matter? I don't know what I was thinking.

A few more weeks went by, and I was due to start my cycle, but I didn't. I was packing to leave for Put-in-Bay with my friends. I called my mom and told her. I said, "Mom, I have a bad feeling I am pregnant."

She said, "Really, I don't think so. Your sister had to go on fertility pills. You will probably have a hard time getting pregnant like she did." Then she said, "Well, she did sell all her baby items in her garage sale. You probably are." My mom blamed my sister for my pregnancy—to her, I got jinxed. My sister and I still laugh about that. At the time, it wasn't funny.

I was off to Put-in-Bay, and I picked up three friends, and we headed down. Ironically, everyone was asking if anyone had a tampon. I had brought many with me, expecting to start my period. On the way home, I finally asked them, "Have any of you had a pregnancy scare?"

Two of the three said yes. I told them I was worried. Wilma offered to go into a drug store to buy me a pregnancy test since I was too embarrassed. She was the first drop-off and had a rather large bathroom, so we all went in. I peed on the stick, and they had me turn around. It took forever.

I was thinking, "What is going on?" I turned around, and they were all pointing at each other—like, "You tell her, no you tell her." Nobody wanted to tell me that it was positive. I slid down the wall, crying, thinking there was no way this could be happening. I dropped the other two girls off and bought two more pregnancy tests. Of course, they both came up positive.

I called George. He came over, and I told him, even though my sister told me not to, or at least to wait. Three and a half months later, when I was four and half months pregnant, we got married. We had a beautiful $40,000 wedding, each side of the family paying $20,000 to host an elaborate 350-person wedding. How many homeless people could we have housed and fed that year? The excess and waste is disgusting, isn't it? I remember I wanted a wedding because I wanted pictures to show my son. Also, I wanted to get married so people at work didn't talk about my getting pregnant and not being married. I did want to try for a family too. I thought that since this happened, it must be God's plan, it must be who God wants me to marry. I do remember saying to my friend on the phone, "If it doesn't work out, I will just get a divorce. I have to give it a try." Isn't that sad? It seems to be how most of society views marriage, if they even consider marriage at all.

I had a son, and he has been the best thing that ever happened to me. He was the beginning of my turnaround. I learned not to be so selfish. I had someone else to take care of; I didn't have just my-self to think about anymore. What I thought was the worst thing that could have happened to me turned out to be the best. I think all babies are planned by God. Nobody is a mistake, and nobody should be treated as one. For, that is what I heard, in so many words, as I was growing up. My dad had a chant he taught me to sing when his friends were over. "I was made because of Kenyon's, I was made at night, I was made in a hurry, and God forgot to make me right." Kenyon's was a bar on the lake where we spent the summers at our lake house. Also there was another little chant. I was often told, "The best part about you ran down your mother's leg." These were all jokes, and I tried to take them as such but I came to realize they bothered me. I never realized as I was growing up that my dad often joked about sex in front of me.

Six

BACKBONE

"Trust in the Lord with all your heart, on your own intelligence rely not; In all your ways be mindful of Him and He will make straight your paths.   Be not wise in your own eyes, fear the Lord and turn away from evil."

Proverbs 3:5-7

Through my marriage, I began to realize things about my childhood and my father, and to relate how I was treated as a child with how I was treated in my marriage. It was the first time I started not to have my dad on the pedestal that I had kept him on for the first thirty years of my life. Then, as in my relationships, he came crashing down as this horrible person and father as all these painful realizations came to the surface. My father was very critical and raged at me at times, times that I don't think a little girl deserved, just as in my marriage. I remember my dad telling me as a teenager, "Promise me you will never be a bitch. There is nothing worse than a bitch of a woman in this world." My dad tries not to deal with a woman in any way, as far as a lawyer, accountant, or bank advisor, etc. I think maybe a woman was really mean to him growing up; I'm not sure. I tried really hard to keep his promise—too hard. I never wanted anyone to think that of me. But sometimes people can bring the worst out in us, and I saw a different side of myself during my marriage.

I remember the day my dad said to me, "You don't have a relationship with that man, and you never will." Shortly after I got married, I sold my house, and George sold his condo. I was staying up north at my parents' house for a couple of months during the summer. George was staying at his friends' place, and he would come up on the weekends. We had a cookie-cutter house built and were waiting for it to be completed so we could move in. My dad didn't want me to go through with it. I said, "I am not ready to give up yet." My baby was only two months old. My dad saw our lack of relationship. I hadn't yet. I felt it, or I should say I have never in my life felt what it is like to have a real and healthy relationship. It's probably another reason why I am so in love with the Lord. I finally have a relationship where I feel someone loves me unconditionally and wants to spend time with me—all I have to do is love Him back and spend quiet time alone with Him.

It was from my marriage that I drew close to God. He was the only one I had who understood my pain, the only one who I felt comfort from. I began to trust Him. I rested in Him; it was the only rest I had. I realized that compared to what I went through with Craig, I had jumped from the frying pan into the fire—just as I was told my grandmother had done—my mom's mom—when she divorced and remarried. Even though mine was an engagement, it was basically the same thing. I was thinking I would stay until my son turned eighteen years old. Then it became twelve, and then it went to eight years old. I waited until just before my son's second birthday to serve my husband papers, which doesn't seem long to be married to someone, less than two and a half years. In that time, I had become unrecognizable to myself and those close to me of who I was once was. I walked on eggshells when he was home. He caused me a lot of pain. I could get away from his pain and get away from him. I feel I left my son to be with that pain every other weekend and every Wednesday night. I didn't protect my son from his father.

I think my son's dad is happier with us not being married, so maybe it isn't so bad. He represented my wounds from my childhood as I represented his. We attract in the positive and negative traits of our parents or care givers, usually more of the negative traits. Through our relationships we are to work through things and heal. Author Harville Hendrix explains this in the book *Getting the Love You Want: A Guide for Couples*. Maybe if my ex and I had realized this, we could have both gone to rehab together and worked on our issues so that our marriage could have worked. At the time, I didn't know I was an addict, and even though recently I told him about my addiction and experience at rehab, I don't think it really shed any light on his darkness. Who am I to judge? Maybe he isn't an addict. I know he has a lot of pain, though. Once I served him papers, he became less controlling, my life no longer felt like a Lifetime Movie—except for a few times during the two and half years together that we lived in the same house after our divorce. We continued to live together because we didn't have the house sold. The market was dropping faster than we could lower the price to match what houses were selling for. Well, my ex-husband was controlling that. I don't think he was ready for us to go our separate ways. We were splitting the bills, living as roommates. It was better, though, for my son and me. My ex was less controlling, yet we were not sharing time with my son yet. It wasn't until my son was four and half that my ex moved out. Looking back, it was a blessing from God that we continued living together as a family longer than planned. God knew it would have been too hard for me to share time with my son at the age of two. At least at four he could talk. It wasn't until my son was five that his dad took him on the regular court-appointed schedule. I then dove into painting every room in my house and being the perfect neat-freak that I was. It was how I coped with the time away from my son.

Around the time my son turned eight, he kept asking me why his father, George and I had gotten divorced. I didn't know what to say. Out of respect to my son and George, I didn't want to give him the gory details, just as I am leaving them out of this book. George is a part of him, and I have to love his father to truly and completely be able to love my son unconditionally, the way every person needs and deserves to be loved. I was unable to do that until my conversion. God gives us the grace to love people who otherwise without Him are hard or even impossible for us to love. I told my son, "Sometimes when your friend comes over and you fight, aren't you happy he has his own house to go home to? You still like your friend and want to see him, but to avoid fighting it is best to be able to take a break from spending so much time together." He still didn't get it and had hoped we would get back together. A year or so later, I was at his dad's house picking him up, and his dad said something that made me angry. Then his dad was joking around and said something like, "We are going to call the police on your mama." I don't even remember why. My blood started to boil, and I said, "What are you talking about?" We didn't even raise our voices at each other, but when my son got in the car, he started to cry.

I said, "What is wrong?"

He said, "I know why you and daddy got divorced now."

He saw something that day that exchanged between his dad and me that had him lose hope in our ever reconciling. It crushed me to know my son was crushed. Maybe he saw how his dad could push my buttons (wounds) like pushing the buttons on a phone. I felt I let him down. Or maybe it was a blessing for him to finally see reality. His dad and I get along really well now; the bitterness we had for each other is gone—or at least it is on my end. As for my son, we got divorced when he was so young, he doesn't remember the fighting. Either way, it was really confusing for him around the age of eight. My counselor told me it was because at eight, children stop being focused on themselves so much and start to notice more of what is going on around them. He was noticing that most of the kids on our block had a mom and dad that lived in the same house. So having two houses wasn't as cool to him anymore as it was when he was younger.

"Do not let your hearts be troubled. You have faith in God; have faith also in me." (John 14:1)

The type of guys I attracted did not respect

my time or what I wanted or how I felt. And when I did voice my opinion, which wasn't very often, I got no validation. Instead, it was like it got shoved back down into myself somewhere. It got ignored, like I hadn't really said anything. It didn't occur to me that that was wrong. But the anger did build up inside like a slowly brewing storm. My adult life was a version or a repeat of my childhood. I gave my power away. As a child I felt powerless, and as an adult I reenacted the story of my youth, even though I couldn't see that is what I was doing. Maybe some parents think children should not have a voice or an opinion. You are creating a disaster for their adult relationships. Children are human beings and deserve to be heard and have a voice with an opinion that is respected. You know best and when to say no to things, but still, they deserve to be listened to and to have their feelings validated! I can't express that enough. How you treat your child is how someone all grown up is going to treat the adult version of your child. For through our partners in life, we try to "fix" and "heal" our childhood wounds, and that goes for everyone—whether they accept that and see it or not.

Because I had "the disease to please," I could never say no. Maybe a weak no or a nah. But when I heard "come on" or "you can" or "please for a little bit," the begging or pleading or coercion made me give in. I usually felt resentful afterward—more ticked at myself than at them. I was the wrong one. I was the weak one who gave in, time and time again. I felt everyone was smarter than me and had it all together more than I did. I wanted to be like them. Deep down, I wanted to be strong and get people to do what I wanted them to do. I envied their power and control. I wanted some of that. The only way I could get that was through sex. I felt powerful. I didn't think I was good at anything else. I liked sex, I thought. No—correction—I loved it, I thought. But what I loved was the power it brought. I felt I could get a man to love me that way. It was the only time I saw them as weak. But it was always short-lived, the sexy dressing and doing what they wanted me to do before they asked. If I did it before they asked, then it was less humiliating. I could feel I was a step ahead of them. But I was the loser because I felt bad afterward. I would get attached and want to turn it into a relationship if we didn't already have one. When it did become a relationship, it was fragile. It was built on nothing more than an addiction, which I didn't realize I had at the time.

I was trying to heal my wounds. Subconsciously, I felt that if these men could love me, then it would heal that wound that I could never mend with my dad. I could never please him enough. I could never be smart enough or work hard enough or accomplish enough. But with sex, I saw these men were satisfied, and they were happy and pleased with me. I did not realize this for twenty years of doing the same thing over and over again, but just with different faces. I didn't get it until I'd spent nearly ten thousand dollars on therapy—my savings. It's what a week at an outpatient rehab facility and a couple of years in counseling every week will buy you these days. I can say that I am so thankful for my awareness. It was worth every penny I spent on it. I couldn't go to my grave not sharing this, even though it is very humiliating. I know there are so many out there like me. Not exactly like me; different wounds make for different versions and variations and twists to the story. We hide our pain from ourselves and others, through the darkness of our false self. We don't know it's not who we really are. It's hard to see our own issues. Yet, it's so easy sometimes to see others' issues, isn't it? The only way I could see my own darkness was by standing in God's light.

I stressed myself out meeting the demands of the men I attracted. I had a few girlfriends that I stressed out trying to meet their demands as well, although it was hardest to get the demanding friends out of my life. They had been a part of my life for so long. I needed to get to the source as to why I was attracted to them. I had to change myself and stop trying to change them. I needed an awareness to recognize them and heal so I could stop wanting the type of person who sucked the life out of me. I learned that I will always be attracted to them, but now, being aware, I can turn my head the other way. I have a voice and an opinion, and I am no longer afraid to use them. That is my greatest asset against most of the men I would usually attract. They do not want anyone with a voice or a strong opinion. They want someone they think of as weak. They look at us like prey, like a coyote spotting a wounded little animal. They marvel at their cunning and their approach and the win. It feeds the huge ego they live behind. I used to think these people were monsters. But they are God's children too. I used to hate them until I learned that "Love thy neighbor" commandment. Now I pray for them.

We can heal and get away from them. Their recovery is longer and it is harder work for them, if they ever get there at all. They truly are the hardest people to love. Yet they need the most love. They always love themselves but in a superficial way, only when things are going well; when something goes wrong, they fall. They fall hard into the pit. It is very hard for them to climb out. I know; I spent a lot of time in the pit, too. But the longer and harder the fall, the more it will hurt. Their pain is so much greater than ours. I am not saying to try to fix them, because that is how most of us get into the messes we get into in the first place. I am saying that part of your healing once you forgive yourself is to forgive them and realize they are also wounded children of God. When people are pushy and aggressive and chase us, we think, wow, they really like us. It's just that they have their own agenda, and it may not be in our best interests. It may be a selfish one. Usually, as my friend stated, "The victims remain victims, and the bullies remain bullies." How about we seek our Healer, Jesus, and become healthy? The problem is that the most wounded of souls think everyone else has the problem, not them. There are easygoing types of men. I know because I dated one at the most wounded time of my life, and I treated him like most of the men I dated had treated me. I looked at him as weak, and his weakness made me boss him around and not like him. I have since apologized to him several times. I treated him horribly.

The easygoing, shy guy was a twenty-five-year-old virgin. I found that out later, after we broke up; he told me as he cried. I was looking in the mirror. I had used sex to get him to like me when I didn't have to. He was different from the others. He didn't push to have sex with me, so I thought he didn't like me. Here he was, a virgin, and he didn't want to have sex within the first few weeks of our relationship, which I didn't understand at all. He was a big challenge to me because I thought he didn't like me. Then once I had sex with him in order to feel loved, I came to view him as a weak man. I had complained about the controlling men in my life, and how I never wanted to be in that situation again, only to find myself at the other end of the spectrum. I almost felt that was worse in a different way. I was so mean to him. I expected him to be a mind reader and know what I wanted. I had a nice guy who would have been nice, but he had sadness in a different way than the others. I was so wounded from my experience when I was engaged, and he was my rebound guy. It was the first time I realized I had become that which I hated in my other failed relationships. It was not that I really had become them; it was more that what was buried in me came to the surface. I couldn't see that was the reason why I had attracted what I had attracted all those times. God was trying to show me why I needed to be healed, but I wasn't getting it. Each guy brought into my life was trying to make it clearer, but I was refusing to see.

The type of guys I usually like know what they want and get mad when they can't have it. They will manipulate and coerce and make you feel guilty. Well, your guilt is already there. They just ignite it from another old wound. They will get you to give in. Then you will feel so ticked off afterward. Pay attention to your feelings. Why are you doing what you are doing? More importantly, how do you feel before, during, and after? Write it down and read it back. These people think everything is about them. You can't just say, "Tonight doesn't work for me." They can't respect that. That doesn't work for them; they have no boundaries. I didn't have any respect for myself and had no boundaries for myself, either. Healthy people with healthy respect and boundaries don't understand how hard it is for us to say "no." They say, "Just tell them no." They don't understand that I couldn't. It had been drilled into me to be obedient and do what I was told from a young age. There are woman who are strong and who are attracted to weaker men, the men with my personality. It goes both ways.

I spent eighty dollars in a counseling session just yelling the word "no," louder and louder and louder. My homework was to go home, look in a mirror, and yell it loudly over and over again. My other homework was that when someone asked me to do something, I had to have a note in front of me to say, "I'll get back to you." That was another eighty dollars in order to learn that if I can't say "no," then I need to carry a note around to tell them "let me think about it" or "I will get back with you" but never to say "yes" automatically. Because "yes" is what my automatic reply was to everything. I didn't want anyone to be mad or think I was not a nice person. I didn't want to disappoint anyone. Each time I did this, the anger got buried. It has to be dealt with in some way. Pick your addiction. Every family that suffers from addiction has their favorites.

When I went to rehab, they had me fill out a family tree, but not the typical kind. I had to fill out aunts, uncles, and cousins back to my grandparents on both sides. Then I filled in each person's addiction. It was easier than you'd think it would be. Once you are enlightened about your own addiction, it is pretty easy to spot the others. It's amazing that it is never talked about. We only talk about the good things, our accomplishments. Who wants to talk about their pain? People don't identify or deal with their pain. Addiction equals pain; you deal with the pain, and you are able to deal with the addiction. First you have to admit you are an addict. Wow, admit you are an addict. Even a small addiction hurts big. You don't have to miss work and mess up your family's life to realize you are an addict. Misery can be a huge indicator of addiction.

You can have a very functional life and still be an addict. At least I could. Especially when you are a sex addict; it is a double life. You can compartmentalize everything. I have my job I am good at. I am a mom, which I try to be good at. I am a daughter, a sister, and a friend, and I try to be there for others—but I'm not very good at that. Then there was my love life, which was really my sex life. It was separate from everything else. My monster was always growing. Where would I be today if Jesus hadn't stopped it? What do you do too much of? What do you try to control? What do you think about and talk about? I can pick up people's addictions just by listening to them talk. I don't even have to see it. When I used to get sad, stressed, or angry, I would masturbate. When I felt lonely and empty, I would look for a boyfriend. In my twenties, I went to the bar with my girlfriends to dance, and it always made me sad to see all of the couples there. I never went out to enjoy my friends. It started out as wanting to see my friends, but once out, it turned into an agenda of hoping to meet "Mr. Right."

I didn't realize it was a problem—until twenty years flew by, and I was single, divorced, and a mom, and I realized I'd had sex with many partners. I think when I was stressed, sad, or lonely, I acted out more. "Acting out" is an addict term. Let's do it in terms everyone understands. I hooked up more. Over those twenty years, I saw no correlation between times of depression or stress and the number of partners I had. So young people may start out with a partner here and there through relationships, but what will it evolve into over time? We have good and evil in us until we get the evil guy off of us. I didn't know he was hooked onto me like an octopus or a bloodsucker, sucking the life out of me, and all the while growing bigger. It took months and months of Christian meditation before I was able to work my way out of his clutches. Even after that, he is still prowling about, seeing where he can get through one of the cracks and come back in.

Even growing up Catholic, I thought about God but never thought about the other guy, the evil one. Here I was feeding that guy like crazy. All the while I was asking God for help. Over the years I know He was there for me even through all that madness. I am so surprised He didn't leave and look at me as a lost cause. The cool thing about God is that He never gives up on us. Never, ever, ever does He give up on us! I never knew how much darkness I was in, and I never realized how much He could help. If I had, I would have tried to stop long ago. He has a plan for all of us. Sometimes He has us go through suffering to get to that rainbow on the other side. His plan is perfect. When He gets to a certain part in the plan, then you can say, "Ooh, I get it now!" But for most of the plan, He had me wondering if He even remembered that He created me. That is the stuff faith is made of, my friends. He was waiting for me, patiently waiting for me to want to kill the monster of love and sex addiction that was inside of me.

> "When you look for me, you will find me. Yes, when you seek me with all your heart, you will find me with you, says the Lord, and I will change your lot." (Jeremiah 29:13-14)

It's interesting to me to be somewhere and to be attracted so strongly to someone. I pray for them as I know they have wounds similar to mine. I have a Healer I can spend time with to receive healing when the wounded child in me gets brought back to the surface. I think of the others who have no idea they even have a wounded child living in them—those who have no idea that their Heavenly Father is watching over them with outstretched arms, waiting for them to turn to Him and say, "Father, please forgive me." There is a loving father, as in the story of the prodigal son in my favorite book, *The Return of the Prodigal Son*, by Henri Nouwen. That book was a life changer for me. Once I knew my Heavenly

Father loved me and forgave me and was there to help me, it started my love affair with the divine, to know that Jesus could heal me of all the pain I had inflicted on myself in my life. Little by little, tears and tears and more tears were all healing me of my past. He was remaking me new into the seedling of a holy person. I didn't have to become a nun or a priest. My greatest treasures became the times of silence with my Lord. Christian meditation got me through the levels of brick wall that I had built up to protect myself from ever feeling the pain of life. Those bricks had also kept me from loving or being loved. Brick by brick, my Savior took down the wall I had built around myself. He replaced it all with His love. I fell deeper and deeper in love with Him. The hurt and pain were replaced with thankfulness and gratitude to Him for saving me from myself. Before that, I had just been doing the best I could to stay alive. I had lived in a dark world of pain and regret, and He took it all away and wiped the slate clean. When I used to think of myself, the word "ho" came to mind, as in slut. Now the word "holy" comes to mind when I think of myself. I can't tell you how great that feels. It took a long time; the evil one wanted to keep those thoughts in my head and remind me of all the dirty things I had done. Then I see Jesus on a cross, bleeding to death, and

I remember He already paid the price for my sins. I don't have to carry them around, for I am truly sorry for them. It's all He wants for us, to be sorry and to seek his help. Once you make that change, your reward is to feel His warm light on your soul. It's better than any warm, sunny, summer day.

The evil one can deceive you. "With closest custody, guard your heart, for in it are the sources of life." (Proverbs 4:23) For most of my life I felt like a victim preyed upon by men. I see it differently now. The say there are three sides to every story. You have heard my side. Yet you have not heard their side. How I have hurt them? The third view I see now is from what could be called God's view. He saw two souls hurt and wounded. Through each other, they were trying to heal their wounds, unknowingly just causing more pain for each other. All of those men in my life were a piece of the puzzle. Life is so puzzling, isn't it? It is in fact a mystery. Just as our Heavenly Father is a mystery. He creates us, and we then inherit personality traits of our parents. This is natural, and it happens this way for everyone. Then we are nurtured or not so nurtured by our caregivers, either our biological parents or adoptive parents. What we get are wounded people with certain personality traits doing the best that they can to raise us. This is why it almost appears as if history repeats itself. The mother who is physically abused by the father has two children, a son and a daughter. The son and daughter grow up either to be abusive to a partner or to be abused to some degree by a partner unless they are able to break the cycle. Families like to keep things hidden, so not much of this may be talked about. Or it could be verbal and emotional abuse, which is harder to see and define. There are no bruises for evidence. We tend to justify it by saying we deserve it or by just not even realizing that there is anything wrong with the situation. It is what we know. Others can see it, but unless you get perspective, you won't see it. Usually the victim, for some reason, tends to protect the abuser or place him or her on a pedestal.

Until I was thirty, all I did was talk about how wonderful and hard-working my dad was. I only stood up to him once, when I was twenty-five. I was having work done at my house by a guy I worked with. He was going to finish the work while I was up north over the weekend at my parents' house. He wanted me to pay him before I left. I talked to my dad about it, and he told me to wait to pay him until the work was done. My dad had been burned before by people who didn't finish work once he had paid them, so he was just trying to help me with his advice and experience. The guy brought it up again and really wanted the money before I left for the weekend. Since I worked with him, and other people from my job recommended him, I figured it would be OK to pay him. It was Friday night of Father's Day weekend, of all weekends. My sister brought it up in front of my dad, asking, "So did you pay that guy?" My dad overheard me say yes, and he flipped out on me. I am nearly as tall as he is, and I got right in his face and blew up right back at him. I told him that because of him I could get talked into anything. That because of him I would do anything anyone asked me to do—anything. It was like twenty-five years of pent-up rage and anger came spewing out, just like at the end of my relationships. He said to me, "There's the door, don't let it hit you in the ass." Same thing he said to me as a teenager. He went up to his barn where he keeps his cars. I was going to go home, and my mom said, "Don't leave; he will be back soon, and he will act like nothing is wrong." She was right—that was exactly what he did. That was what he always did, and it was so confusing to me.

Even now that I'm forty, he will look at me and say in front of my nieces, "There is someone only a mother can love." All I can do is pray for him and think he is missing out on a great relationship with me. I refuse to search any longer, looking for a man to fill that void. After all, now I have heaven. It hurts and reopens those old wounds, but this time I have somewhere to rest my wounded soul, in Jesus's arms. My Heavenly Father loves me, even if I can't get my biological father to love me. Maybe he is too wounded to do so. I'm OK now, and soon you will be too. What helped me to forgive my father for not being able to love me in the way I needed him to love me was an Unbound conference I went to at Our Lady of Good Counsel. It was amazing. Neal Lozano wrote a book and created the conference on the five keys of getting unstuck and delivered from the darkness of the evil one and staying connected to God. He was not at the one I went to, as he travels all over the world doing them. It released me of the pain I had toward my father. I was forgiven for not loving my dad the way God wants me to love him, which is unconditionally. It released me from my prison sentence created by me of blaming my father for the way my life had turned out. I was healed from so many of the serpent's lies about myself. It was in November of 2014. I realize that healing is perpetual and that you can always go deeper.

My mom tells me all the time, "Your father never listens to me; he does what he wants and acts like a single man." That is exactly how I felt about most of the guys in my life, even when I was engaged or married. During the week of rehab, they told me to be less like my mom. My mom's parents got divorced when she was two. Her dad moved back to Canada so he didn't have to pay child support. Her three siblings went into the orphanage, and her mom's sister—Aunt Loretta to her and to us—took her in until her mom got her life together, which to her mom meant getting remarried. My mom loved it at Loretta's house. Loretta left her family farm in Saginaw and hitchhiked at the age of thirteen to Muskegon. I don't know why she left. Eventually my mom went back to her mom's house when her siblings got out of the orphanage. My mom told me her sisters liked it at the orphanage, and the oldest wanted to stay. From that point on, though, she was the only one of her four siblings (her mom had a child with her stepdad) to spend every summer near Lake Michigan at Aunt Loretta's house in Muskegon. She even called home once to ask her mom if Aunt Loretta could adopt her. She said that when she heard her mom's voice, she couldn't do it. She said no matter how your parents are, they are your parents, and you love them. She said her stepdad was very controlling and made her eat all the food on her plate. My mom's favorite thing in the world to do is eat out and eat good food.

Now that my mom has a backbone, my dad tells me she is a bitch. She jokingly tells him it is payback for all of the years she never spoke up. My dad gets upset with anyone, even my mom, if we have a different opinion from his or call him out on something. He is easily wounded and highly sensitive to anything that could even remotely be viewed as criticism. Even though his dad worked several different jobs at once, his family was very poor. Growing up, they owned and lived in a boarding-house with renters. My mom told me my dad said he saw a lot go on there with the tenants. The kids' room was upstairs with the tenants. The only story I know is that he saw a man beat up his wife and then throw her down the stairs. He and his three siblings shared a room. His dad was very easygoing and had a big beer belly from drinking. He was so sweet to me and called me "Sunshine" or "Good morning" instead of Dawn. I never remember anything but his kindness. I think he was a lot like my mom, minus the drinking. His name was Carl, and my dad told me his father grew up on a tobacco farm in Kentucky and ran away from home at the age of thirteen. I don't know why he left. My dad's mom... well, they think she had something mentally wrong with her. She would never give them lunch money the night before school, but if my dad woke her up for some in the morning, she would yell terribly at him. She would let him stay home from school if he would clean her house. She had been married prior to my grandfather Carl. Her mom had been divorced too. I don't know the stories as to why.

My father only went to school up to the eighth grade; he had dyslexia, though he didn't know it at the time. Nobody knew about that stuff back then. I see many of the girls at the pregnancy center with what appear to be learning disabilities. They have dropped out of high school and don't like to read. Some ask me to fill out their forms because they can't spell well. It costs me and my son's father $440 a month to take my son to the reading and language arts center for his tutoring twice a week, due to his dyslexia. He has been a year behind in his reading since first grade. He was held back in kindergarten. He was diagnosed with dyslexia at the end of first grade. The school assured me they could help. They do work with him, and he goes to a resource room teacher to help with his reading. Yet she doesn't know Orton-Gillingham, which is how he needs to learn.

The Orton-Gillingham approach teaches directly and systematically the language elements that non-dyslexic learners acquire easily. One element is that dyslexics have to learn the 34 spelling rules. For example, one rule is, in order to put a past tense on the word hop, they learn to double the 'P' whenever a consonant is not protected by another consonant. A dyslexic would typically spell the word hop in a past tense form by adding "ed", without doubling the "P" and not know the word is now hoped and not hopped. It is very detailed and takes repetition for the spelling rules to sink in as the dyslexic usually has a low working memory. They have to practice what they learn. She doesn't understand why he doesn't want to write, which is common with children who have dyslexia, since they don't know how to spell, yet this is the only help we have. I e mailed her about watching a fifty-minute video I have on dyslexia, but I never got a response. This is who I have to rely on to help my son. My son tells me only one teacher has liked him—funny thing, that teacher had dyslexia. Our school system lives without God, and it shows in the level of compassion that our children get for the issues that they have no control over. His father and I started him at the tutor since he has not made progress to get caught up, consistently staying a year behind in reading for three years now. The other three children in the subdivision where I live who have dyslexia are carpooled to a special school to help them with their dyslexia. That school is forty-five minutes away, and it costs over $20,000 a year.

According to Austin Learning Solutions, 20 percent of school-aged children are dyslexic, and over forty million American adults are dyslexic, but only two million know it. It does not mean the people who have dyslexia are not smart, over 50% of the NASA employees are dyslexic. It just means we have to step up and care enough to test every child who shows signs of it, first all of the teachers would have to know the signs and name it and then teach them to read and write the way in which they learn. I have spoken to so many people who have it and they all tell me they felt so much better once they knew what it was. I had an engineer friend who was diagnosed with it in his thirties tell me, "I no longer felt stupid once I knew I had dyslexia". Over and over again I hear once it is named those who had dyslexia felt a relief to know why they struggled the way they did.

My son has a hard time getting his thoughts on paper. I was told by the dyslexia clinic that he will have to dictate his papers for me to write them out, and then he can copy it. It's too hard for him to do both. It's easy to judge the kids who do poorly or drop out of school. I know I did until I had this experience with my son. He had a wonderful reading teacher in first grade who told me to have him tested. I wish all teachers had her level of compassion. Usually his teacher is frustrated because he won't write very much. I have to advocate for him and remind the teacher about his dyslexia and what is involved and what it means to have dyslexia. I was told by the lady at the dyslexia clinic that school is twice as hard for him. What about the people who don't know any of this? I used to yell at him for not wanting to read. I was so mean to him—just as other parents don't know and do the same. I was blindly wounding my child. Heaven's gifts of patience, love, and kindness are beautiful gifts that we all need for those we interact with in our lives, especially our children. Before I had my healing, I used to view my life as overwhelmingly hard. When we are healthy, life doesn't seem as hard. Plus, God gives us the grace we need to have peace in the storm.

Seven

LAST RELATIONSHIP

"For while your obedience is known to all, so that I rejoice over you, I want you to be wise as to what is good, and simple as to what is evil; then the God of peace will quickly crush Satan under our feet. The grace of our Lord Jesus be with you."

Romans 16:19-20

I write this book as a working shepherd of the Lord, hoping to help bring His flock of sheep back home. If it weren't for God I would never have known I was a sex and love addict. Nobody told me I was until I went to counseling. It was by God's grace that I went to counseling and to the right counselor who could help me. It was hard to be honest with her at first. Well, it was hard to be honest with myself. As I sat and told her why I was there, to have a long term relationship, I was trying to end things with my boyfriend, Marty, but we would keep ending up back together. I just wasn't happy though. It was fun hanging out with him, but nothing else clicked. We were just good at having fun together. We would have a few cocktails, hang out, and watch a movie or go and listen to a band on the weekends when we didn't have our kids. We had great sex; all that was fine. But that was all it was. That was all we had. I felt empty as usual, and I was looking to him to fill me up, which was an impossible expectation, because at the time I was a bottomless pit. At first it was awesome, but then I just felt like he wasn't really there for me.

I felt that his phone calls were made out of duty. He was into me when it was convenient for him and when he felt like seeing me, which was typical of my relationships prior to my marriage. This was my first relationship after my divorce. I didn't want a man around my son, so at first I thought it was great that he felt the same regarding his kids. But then after time, it kind of became obvious that I felt used for sex. I felt used because I didn't feel loved. The relationships I was in were built on the fun and excitement—not out on care and compassion and love of a true partner. I didn't know how to give that kind of love, so I got back what I gave, which was superficial love. I attracted what I was. God puts people in our lives like mirrors, so we can try to see who we are through the people we interact with. But instead, we just see their faults instead of recognizing our own in them.

I met Marty through my hairdresser. She had two very different prospects in mind. One wanted kids and the other didn't. So she set me up with the one who didn't want kids. Plus, I had told her I just wanted someone to "hook up" with (have sex with). It took me a few sessions to be honest with myself and my counselor, and to tell her that. I was lonely, and I wanted companionship and to have fun. I was not looking to get involved with anyone in a committed, serious way. Was I ever? I think Marty knew that coming in. While on our second date, he said, "Tell me we are going to have sex tonight." I said, "We are going to have sex to-night," as I swallowed a lump in my throat. Then on the way back to his place, I remember looking out the car window and crying, thinking, "Here I go again." It was going to start up again, even when I told myself that I didn't really know what "it" was.

I think my soul knew I was an addict before I could stop the denial and admit it. Deep down I knew the pain that it would bring. But wasn't this what I wanted? Wasn't this what I had signed up for? That night felt painful to me—all of it. It was awkward and uncomfortable. But as always, once I slept with someone then I turned into a clingy girl. Ironical-ly, our song became "Addicted," by Saving Abel. I felt that, to justify what I had done, I had to turn it into a relationship to make myself feel better. I have talked with other sex addicts, and they usually don't want to see the person again after they have sex. Or they just want to escape and get away right after. But for me, this was when the fantasy would start.

Marty hunted, so suddenly I was OK with eating deer meat. Marty wasn't into eating out for dinner but was OK with going out for drinks, so I was OK with going out for drinks and not going out to dinner. I would get all showered and shaved up just like the Bible scripture in Ezekiel 23:40: "And so for them you bathed yourself, painted your eyes, and put on ornaments." We got into a routine of seeing each other every other weekend when we didn't have our children. We hung out and had a blast together. We had both come out of painful marriages and were like two wounded birds trying to help with the other's wounds. All we were doing was medicating ourselves with alcohol and sex, but it was nothing that anyone would consider an addiction. We were just enjoying life—or so I thought. This kind of enjoyment takes you down a path of destruction. It is just delaying the pain, which only makes it worse.

I thought this time it would be different. This was the one. I soon fell head over heels in love (lust), just as with all the others. I thought I could get him to love me, not knowing at the time that not everyone is capable of love, including myself. As time went by, a light bulb came on for me: I realized he wasn't over his ex-wife and all of that pain. My world came crashing down. I crash-landed and hit rock bottom, or so I thought. I told him I wasn't happy, but he was different from the others. He tried to help. He proposed to me with a beautiful engagement ring. I again said yes right away, but by the end of the day, I told him I couldn't and gave him the ring to take back to the store.

He found a counselor that I liked. After I told her about our back-and-forth and up-and-down relationship, she pointed out that you can be addicted to someone. I said, "Really? I had never heard of that." She said, "It is called love addiction." The way counseling works is that they drop little hints and then you look into it and dig into it and figure stuff out for yourself. I looked it up, and it explained why I had a hard time breaking up with guys. Even when I knew they weren't right for me and didn't like them, I would see them again and have sex with them when I saw them. So the pieces of the puzzle were starting to fit together. I didn't realize that Marty was covertly controlling. I didn't realize it until he would show up at my door unannounced, even after we broke up, and I would answer the door and we would hang out and end up having sex.

My counselor said, "Why do you answer the door? Since once you answer the door you end up having sex with him?"

I said, "I felt bad." I know that is hard to believe, but remember, I was not mentally healthy at this point in my life. I had a sickness. The addict in me was so attracted to him, and I think he knew it; he knew if I saw him I would give in. Maybe that was the codependent in me putting other people before me. A few times when it happened, I was able to resist answering the door. With my car in the garage and the garage door shut, he couldn't tell if I was home or not. He knew my schedule. The weekends that I didn't have my son were the same ones he didn't have his kids. By becoming aware, I did learn to realize that even though I felt bad for not answering the door, I felt worse when I answered the door and had sex with him. That would restart the relationship, if you want to call it that. To us, it was a relationship, though now I see it was just sex.

Marty once said, "Even though you say you don't want to see me, I think you do." At the time I didn't understand, but now I get it. When my addict was driving me, I would look at someone with lust, even though the other part of me knew I needed to stay away from him and that it wasn't good for me. It was a battle I wasn't aware of at the time. Looking back, I fought that battle often. Marty once told me that people date to have sex. Not all people do that—just sex addicts date to have sex. Sex addicts have what we call a three-second rule. You don't look at someone for longer than three seconds because otherwise it may spark a fantasy in your head, since that is where most sex addicts live—in their heads. They aren't really present, but nobody would know that. The main part of sex addiction is the fantasy in the addict's head. That is where the main thrill is. The physical hookup is the downer, where you hit bottom and can never be satisfied. It's never enough for the addict. As the monster grows, the monster needs more.

I dated another covert manipulator like Marty in my late twenties. It was the last guy I dated before I met George and got pregnant. His name was Don, and our relationship was a lot like Marty's and mine. It was very sexual. One Wednesday night, I had class for my MBA. Don said, "Get out of class at nine, an hour early. I have a surprise for you at your house." So, being obedient, I didn't ask any questions, and I did what I was told. He had a key to my place and was already inside when I got there. I don't remember if I saw another car in the driveway or if it was out in the street, but there was someone else there. Don had gotten me a girl for my "surprise." I had told him I had a fantasy of a threesome, and he made it happen. Looking back on it now, I think she was a stripper. She had Dolly Parton boobs, and I couldn't believe what was going on. It was surreal. I was shaking, literally shaking. It ended with Don having sex with her. It all happened so fast. Maybe he only had her rented for a half hour; I have no idea. At one point when he looked over at me, it made a shudder run down my spine.

I looked into his eyes, and the only word that came to mind was evil. I wanted to run out of there and get away. I felt so dirty in that moment. I felt such a strong presence of evil that I had never experienced before—until that time or since that time. We broke up after that. I never spoke up to stop any of it.

Again, I just froze and went along with what was going on. A fantasy and reality are two totally different things. I felt he set me up for what was really his surprise with a paid hooker. Shortly after that, my car got rear-ended, and Don let me borrow his car while mine was being repaired. I cleaned up his car in and out before giving it back to him, and I found a key under the console insert when I was vacuuming. Something told me to check it, and it was to my own front door. He must have made another copy of my house key prior to giving it back to me. Before this all happened, one time I had come home from up north, and my house smelled of candles. I asked him, "Did you have someone over?" My living room, bathroom, and bedroom all smelled of candles. He told me it was like I was psychic. Can you believe how stupid I used to be? I guess I shouldn't say that about myself, but why didn't I break up with him then? It's like I ignored it. I ignored so much so often with the men in my life. It doesn't seem possible that I could be so...I don't know...*desperate*? There is no word to describe my lack of self-worth and self-respect. It just shows how sick I was, how sick the men were, and how sick our society is. People don't have a clue. I had a boss tell me once, "You don't really know who I am, just like I don't really know who any of my employees are." Amen to that. Most of us don't really know ourselves, let alone somebody else.

"For God did not give us a spirit of cowardice but rather of power and love and self-control. (2 Timothy 1:7)

In July of 2011, a year before I went to rehab, I went to a weekend seminar, which was basically a weekend of psychology. It was a mini-rehab even though I didn't know it until I went to rehab for a week. I learned that there were sixteen other people besides me, all with different stories, all in pain but with different shades and degrees of it. I learned that when people were children and saw their moms get beat up by their dads, they felt frustrated because they couldn't help. So when they grew up, they tried to control their lives with sex, alcohol, or any number of things. They needed something to be in control of. Yet that addiction was what they lacked control of. I learned that when children are molested, they lose their power and try to regain it in other ways as adults. These tragic events were all the real-life childhoods of those I spent the weekend with. It was the first time I felt unconditional love, and it was the first time I realized I wasn't alone. We were forced to share our pain and stare it in the face. I was forced to see things that I have never seen before about my past. That's who we hide our pain from the most—ourselves.

The psychologist there said, "Do you realize you are going all over town trying to please everyone because you ultimately are trying to please your father?"

I said, "No."

She overheard me tell someone that I said "I love you" to my dad, and he said nothing back. It's how he grew up. I ignored how this affected me and decided that I had to make peace with him. He did the best he could, based on how he was raised and what he didn't get that he needed as a child, which caused his wounds. People don't know that everyone has wounds. The psychologist at the seminar was the first person to explain this to me. In time, I would hear it over and over again. We don't get a manual on what to do and what not to do, geared specifically for our child. Staying wounded doesn't help our children. Nor does parenting the way our parents did.

"Just say no!" Whenever I hear someone say that about someone struggling with a vice, it ticks me off. One of the helpers at the seminar wrote that on my affirmation statement board. We had to make an affirmation statement about ourselves. We wrote down our negative thoughts and then had to turn each word into a positive to come up with a new statement, to replace the negative thoughts we had about ourselves. So my negative thoughts were that, "I am ugly and unworthy, and I hate myself." Instead, the helpers helped me to write out the opposite of those words. My statement became, "I am a self-worthy, beautiful woman, and I love myself just the way I am." In July of 2011, I framed that positive affirmation board and hung it in my bathroom where I could see it in the mirror every morning as I got ready for my day.

I went to take it down recently, and my son said, "Mama, put that back up. Why would you want to take that down?" He doesn't even know what it means to me or why it is there.

My cousin, who was a nun, once told me, "Listen to your child. God will speak through him all the time."

Why would I take it down? I think because I finally believe it and live it each and every day. I chose to take my son's godly advice and leave it up. By leaving it up, it reminds me of how far I have come and how much work I have done on myself to get here. It was worth every minute of my time. Because I matter and I count, and I will stand to make a difference to educate the world on my struggles with sex addiction so those who suffer from it can be free just as I am free of it.

Our actions, and the anxiety and depression we suffer, are all indicators that we have pain that we are burying and that needs to be dealt with. But here is the thing: some don't even know they are in pain. We live in a world where you are in the minority if you're close to God. It is more normal to go out and party and hook up than it is to love God with your heart, mind, body, and soul. I have had more criticism about being close to God than I ever had when I was living my life, going from relationship to relationship.

The pain of staying the same had to be greater than the pain of changing. Now that I have done the work and dealt with the pain and gotten through to the other side, how do I bring the others over? How do I convince them that they have pain that needs to be dealt with? Once they seek Jesus, their lives will be so much better. It sucks to go through the pain and deal with it, but it is so worth it. For God, I gave up my old life and died to my old self, but I have risen brand-new. I have been healed to be a compassionate person who finally respects and loves herself, which in turn allows me to love others the way God does. I used to objectify myself and others. I looked at my size-four body as having too-small breasts and a too-small butt, and my skin had all these freckles and was too white.

I once had a guy tell me I would be hot if I grew my hair long and got tanned and had a boob job and gained a little weight. This guy was my boyfriend. It did upset me, but I took it. He was a skinny, beanpole guy, and he admittedly said, "I know I shouldn't talk, because look at me." This is the man I dated. This is the man I gave myself to. He was as wounded as me, but the male version. He was someone who judged and criticized me just as I did him. I gave myself away to men who didn't care about me, and it made me angry. I had buried anger, and I had hatred for myself because of it. I can't believe I spent nearly all of my life hating myself. I used to live in darkness, unaware of my sin—the sin of trying to medicate my pain, which only caused me more pain. My only way out was to fall in love with the Lord; my true-love experience is with His powerful mercy.

Eight

RECONCILIATION

"Watch carefully then how you live, not as foolish persons but as wise, making the most of the opportunity, because the days are evil. Therefore, do not continue in ignorance, but try to understand what is the will of the Lord."

Ephesians 5:15-17

In the fall of 2011, I learned the term "love addiction." By January I was feeling as if I didn't need counseling anymore. I was good, I had this. I was doing well, not letting Marty into my life, and not seeing him. I thought I was kicking this love addiction thing. Being aware is half the battle, they say. So the other half I could manage—or so I thought. I asked my counselor, "Do you feel like I don't need any more counseling?" She said, "The important thing is that you feel you don't need any more counseling." I knew she thought I needed more counseling, but I didn't go back to counseling until I bottomed out.

I signed up for a retreat at St. Mary's Retreat Center. What a way to start off 2012—with a retreat! I felt God was calling me to it. I can't even remember the topic. First, they handed me the agenda, and I saw that confession would be in half an hour. I literally took one look at the agenda, saw it there in print, and looked back at the door. I thought, "Oh no, get me out of here! Confession?!" Really, I just wasn't ready. It wasn't planned, and I am a planner. I had always planned nearly every detail of every day of my life except my dates. I was sweating, even though it was the dead of winter and not overly warm in the retreat center. I just kept saying to myself, "You can do this, Dawn. You can do this." But could I? What would God think of me?

God already knows everything. Why does it seem overwhelmingly frightful to divulge everything? Then it is true. It means it happened. Living in reality is a part of being mentally healthy. So many of us don't realize we don't live there. So, I got toward the front of the line. I just wanted to get it over with. I think I cut three people off. I was thinking, "I don't care. I can't wait an hour and sit in agony. I have to get it over with; otherwise, I'm afraid I'll drive back home." I was second in line. I didn't have to wait too long for the person in front of me to finish. I was thinking, "Is she a saint? I mean, how long will it take to spill my gut of sin?" I had not been to face-to-face confession since the second grade. Except there was that time I went and told a priest I had premarital sex, but this was another fifteen years later. Now I knew my beast. I was ready to turn my life in another direction.

I sat in a little room, face-to-face with Father Alex. He was a cute priest and close to my age. I was like, "Really, Lord, you are hilarious. Couldn't you have had me do this with a really old priest?

One who's hard of hearing and maybe in need of a pair of nose-hair trimmers?" But nope, so here goes.

I said, "Um, I am kind of an addict, a love addict. I get love and sex confused, and I have had many partners over my life since I was a teenager." I cried and cried, and it was very much a relief. I think my soul finally started to heal from that moment.

A few months later, I asked Father Steve from my parish, "Why do we have the Sacrament of Reconciliation? It is so humiliating."

He said, "Dawn, it is not to humiliate you. Everyone eventually confesses, be it to their sister, friend, or hair dresser."

Good point. Might as well go to a priest and receive absolution and healing from Jesus. I was once introduced to one of the priests at my parish, Father Mike, and I told him, "I have been to you for confession."

He said, which was so cool, "I get paid to forget."

He didn't remember what I went to him to confession for; he didn't even remember me. They see so many people, they can't remember our stuff. It helped me to not be so terribly embarrassed about going to confession, and to realize I was missing the point. The point of it is to be healed and open up the barrier my sins had created to my Lord. It lets His light shine in on us so that the journey of healing can begin. Such a small number of people utilize this gift, yet people wonder why they don't feel close to Him.

Father Alex told me to pray the rosary for my penance and that it would be a good idea to pray the rosary every day. He said, "Prayers to the Blessed Virgin Mary are powerful, and she can help you." He gave me a pamphlet on it and directions about how to do it. He told me about the beautiful pictures next to the prayers. From that day on, I have been praying the rosary. He is right. Praying to the Blessed Virgin Mary was a huge part of loosening the shackles of my addiction, although I didn't realize it at the time.

After the third day at home of praying the rosary, I thought I had seen an apparition of the back of a Blessed Virgin Mary statue that people usually put in their gardens. It was five o'clock in the morning as I walked down the steps from my bedroom. She was in front of my window looking out. I told my family about it when they were over, and then something fell off the mantle above the fireplace—nothing breakable, just an unframed portrait I had resting on the mantle. I had a spiritual director at the time from Manresa, and I told her about it. She said, "The Blessed Virgin Mary will do things like that."

It was the first of many holy mysteries experienced on this journey.

The Blessed Virgin Mary is a big part of my calling. There was a vision I had during prayer—it is at the end of this book. Holy Week of 2013 is when I received the final image that came to me through meditation during my prayer time. It had been just about a year since I had discovered my sex addiction, and June would be the one-year anniversary of my week at rehab. I had come so far and worked so hard. The image or vision—I'm not sure what to call it—was of the Blessed Mother crying and Jesus taking a baby from a pile of babies in a meadow. Jesus put each baby in God's hands, and God our Heavenly Father put angel wings on each baby. They are the aborted babies. God takes them back and makes them angels. It started with a pile of babies in a meadow in March of 2013. I told the priest, Father Sean, from my Catholic2Catholic group about it. I didn't understand what it meant. In a way, I still don't. In time, God will reveal it.

Father Sean said, "If it leads to something good, it was from God. If it leads to something bad, it was from the evil spirit." That really freaked me out. I had never heard that before. Then it all started clicking with my past and all of the things I did that never led to anything good. All those years of sin, when the evil spirit had taken me over, and I didn't even know it! Think of all the others he has taken over, and they don't even know it. People talk about God. We don't want to talk about the evil spirit, of course—for good reasons. I think we need to start so we can become aware of him, and discern what is from him and what is from God.

Each time I prayed, over time, more was added to the picture. Jesus was added, like I said, giving the babies to God the Father who put the wings on them. Then Jesus took me to God the Father, and He put angel wings on me! I never saw His face. He was on a throne sitting there, and Jesus took me to Him. This was so amazing to me. I felt weird telling anyone, though. I am new to acknowledging the spirit world. I think once you have been in the spirit world, after a while these stories seem more believable because you are around more spiritual people, and you hear of more things like this. But at first when this stuff happens to you, you don't know what to think of it. What was that? You kind of keep on the down-low about it.

On Holy Thursday of 2013, I was praying in the morning during my usual prayer time. I hung out with Jesus and did contemplative prayer, and I had the vision again. The Blessed Virgin

Mary was there, and this time she was crying.

She said, "Please help my babies. Please tell the other girls your story."

I didn't hear her audibly. It was a small voice from within. So I started writing in a notebook from that day on. I didn't quite know when I would actually write the book or if it was a book I was supposed to write. I felt after communion at the Good Friday Mass, in a still, small voice I was told to write the book and call it *Ashes to Gold: a Book for People who are Hurting*. All the while I was asking myself, "Really, is this real?" I was communicating with heaven, and they gave me direction to do this. It was so amazing; I was on fire! It is not something you can run out and tell people, which is hard for someone like me, who struggles with boundaries.

Dave, the guy next to me at work is always sketching things at lunch. I thought, "I am going to tell him my vision and see if he can sketch it."

He did it that night at home and brought it in the very next day, and it looked amazing. I didn't realize how talented he was. He added St. Joseph into my picture. He was not there in my vision. Dave is a father of four and a family man. He thought St. Joseph should be in it too. So now I had a picture to make the vision come to life. I kind of had proof of what I saw in my prayer. But now what? I didn't want to mess anything up. So I waited. I had all this stuff in my head that I was supposed to get out, but then what would I do with it? I was not sure how I was going to put it all together or what story I was supposed to tell. All I knew was that Mary was sad, there are thousands of abortions a day, and she wants me to help her. How could I help her babies?

If you have experienced an abortion, please use the image for healing, and know that your baby is in heaven, and you will be re-united again one day. An artist suggested that people could color it with colored pencils, mark-ers, or paint, and use it as art therapy for healing.

"We had all gone astray like sheep, each following his own way; But the Lord laid upon him the guilt of us all." (Isaiah 53:6)

Getting back to the realization, it was February of 2012. Once I was aware of the love and sex addiction, and I had been on retreat and done my general confession, I thought I could handle the addiction, since I didn't really think it was a huge problem. Since I didn't think of dating and having sex with someone you are attracted to as an addiction, even if I'm nearly forty and have had multitudes of partners. I went on another re-treat at my church—just an evening and day thing.

At the Friday evening retreat again, Father Alex was there, and he wasn't even our parish priest. He said to everyone, "The Lord is going to tell you something after you receive the Eucharist."

I'm thinking, "What?" I was newly getting into the spirit world so this didn't make sense to me one bit, but I am an open person, so I went with it. Sure enough, I got this small voice deep within me, saying, "Stay with me." I'm thinking, "Just what does that mean?" That meaning would be revealed a few weeks later.

Going into March of 2012, my friend wanted me to go on a second date with a guy she knew. For the first date, we met at a restaurant, and I was a good girl. I didn't even let him walk me to my car afterward. She called to tell me that he thought I was really guarded. She assured me he was a really great guy.

I said, "No, I don't know, he reminds me of someone I used to date. I don't think I should go out with him again." Slowly I was becoming aware that even though I was attracted to him, he reminded me of someone from my past. I was becoming more aware of my feelings and listening to them.

She and her friend really pushed me to go out with him again, and he called for another date. I tried to explain to him and be up-front that if he was looking for a sexual type of relationship, I was not interested. I wanted to take things really, really slowly, and I was looking for a very long-term relationship, like for the rest of my life. It is sad that I had to explain this, but on the first date he had brought up sex—as most of the guys I had dated do—so I felt that if I were going to go out with him again, I needed to tell him where I stood.

I tried to get him to go out with my other friend instead, one who was really into dating. He suggested meeting for coffee and said that he understood and was fine with how I felt about waiting to have sex. I forget that some people will say anything to get you to do something. We met and talked a lot, and that was the second date. He talked of his financial issues, so for our third date, I offered to make dinner, and we could have some drinks at my house. I would learn in rehab this was my ritual—all sex addicts have a ritual, I would learn. It was hard for me to see that mine was entertaining my dates at my house, drinking alcohol, and playing house. This is where it goes south.

Charles is my "rock-bottom guy." He had a lot to drink. I am not a vodka drinker but had some at my house, and he drank all of it. I drank wine, and we talked for nearly seven hours. I had probably three drinks, and since I typically only drink socially, and since I was not so social anymore, that was too much for me. We started kissing and ended up having sex. This was my rock-bottom moment. For me, it was March 11, 2012: the last time I had sex.

It was so weird that time. I felt so aware of the addiction. Before, I didn't believe I was a sex addict since I never felt this overpowering struggle within myself. I think it was because I had never tried to stop it. I just always went with it. To feel the addiction, I think you need to go against it and not want to give in to it. So there I was—as soon as we got done having sex, I plummeted. Like I was on top of a huge mountain and someone suddenly pushed me off, and I fell all the way down, not just to the ground but farther. I fell into a deep, dark hole—I mean really deep. I was crying and felt so bad, since this was not what I wanted. I thought I was stronger than this. I was devastated.

Before we had sex, he had wanted to stay the night, but after we had sex, he gave some reason why he had to go home. He apologized and felt bad and told me not to be upset, that sex is natural and normal. I have a hard time explaining the pit of hell I was in. He left, and I tried to sleep. The next day I was still in the deep, dark hole. I had never felt this before. Or maybe I had, but I was never as aware of my feelings as I was at that moment. I wanted to masturbate to alleviate the pain and desire I felt. I did, and yet, still I wanted to see him again. I knew this time that he was like the others I had been attracted to in the past. I knew we could try to have a relationship, and I would fall head over heels into a lustful state of thinking he was awesome if I let myself. I would put him on a pedestal for a year or two and try to have a relationship that I would be happy in. But this time I knew how it would end: like all the other times. I would end up telling him what a selfish jerk I thought he was. I would do this once I had nothing left to give of myself to him. I would do this once the lust had worn off and the blinders and masks fell to the floor and the lights were on. I would see that our relationship was basically about sex.

We would try to do normal relationship things, and maybe we would go to movies and eat out. There would be nothing there, though, no compassion toward each other or forgiveness for incidents. Instead there would be a wall built up. In time, I would be too tired to try to take the bricks down one by one. Instead I would blow up the wall with dynamite and say "get out of my life" as I had done to all the others.

I told him and tried to explain this to him, but he said, "No, it won't be like that. It can be different this time."

I said, "It won't. I'm the same girl who has been in all those other relationships, and you are basically the same guy I have attracted all those times. I will have the same experience with you that I had with all of the others. You are a really smart guy who thinks he knows more than everyone else. You have really low self-esteem that you hide with an overinflated ego. I'm the girl who will fan the flames of your ego to make it even bigger and listen to every word you say because I will also think you know everything and are the smartest person. We are the opposite side of each other's coin. We fit together so well. Me, the doormat, and you the strong, domineering, controlling guy who exudes power that I am oh-so-attracted-to."

I really am a strong person, but it is buried, so I never find it. I only find it in the person that I attract. It fits, since I think of myself as "less than." Nobody sees this side of me. I exude a sense that I have it all together. I have a great house and nice car, I'm college educated, with a master's degree, and I have a great job that I work hard at. Deep inside me is a wounded child—the inherited family traits of addiction. I wore a mask so that even I could not see the real me. I could not see the hurting child inside who needed healing. I wanted to start a relationship with Charles, but this time I knew better. I knew it wouldn't be healthy, and I knew I wanted a different life. I knew I needed help.

Thinking back to that retreat at my church, I realize now just what that small voice from God meant when He said, "Stay with me." I had sinned again and put up a wall between myself and God. Yet I also knew God wanted me. He wanted me to stay with His Son, Jesus, the Healer. The Lord had shined a light on my darkness to show it to me. I didn't even know I had lived in this darkness for so long. My Lord didn't want to punish me. He wanted to set me free. He had set me on a path to be free of my chains of addiction and break the family tradition of addiction that had plagued our family for so long.

I went two weeks later for my thirty-eighth birthday to a place called Manresa that offers retreats. I was there to go deeper with God and to enhance my Christian meditation with Father Bernie and learn more about it. But instead of doing that, I had built up a wall of sin from the events that took place with Charles. I prayed and sat and meditated for two days that weekend and never once encountered Jesus or His light. I passed tiny little offices, including one with an open door in which a priest sat at his desk, willing to hear confession at a moment's whim, and all I did was walk on by. My pride overcame my shame and guilt, and I couldn't walk in there and reconcile with the Lord and confess to his servant what I had done. Even though it was someone I would have never seen again. My sin had ruined my birthday plans with my Lord.

A few weeks passed, and a pastoral woman at the church invited me to participate in a foot-washing ceremony at the Holy Thursday Mass. The bishop was coming to do the washing. I had taken a "Called and Gifted" class from the woman, a class on discerning one's spiritual gifts that was based on Sherry Weddell's book, *Forming Intentional Disciples*. I was one of the chosen apostles. I went alone. My son was with his father and all of my family lives an hour or more away. None of my friends were into going to church, even though most were Catholic. I just sat in the pew, crying, waiting for Mass to begin. I felt like a failure and a fraud. I realize now I wasn't a failure and a fraud—I was human, and exactly who God sent His Son, Jesus, to die for. I was trying to be holy and get close to God, but I had failed. I was in my "darkness of the night" hour and in pain. When Bishop Byrnes knelt down to wash my feet, the feet of a sinner, I felt so unworthy. But we are all unworthy of God's mercy and love. It's why He calls it mercy and why His love is so amazing. The beautiful thing is, He gives it to us anyway. He gave it to me in that pew with that holy man looking up at me, looking into my eyes with

God's love penetrating from his soul into mine. A week later, I went to see Father Steve at my church to receive the Sacrament of Reconciliation. I told him what happened with Charles and that I was seeking help. I never once felt an ounce of condemnation from him, only God's love and mercy with my struggles. He saw me crying before Mass, sitting in that pew on Holy Thursday. Our eyes met; he didn't know what pain I was in, but he saw it. Confession is raw beauty, confession is freeing, and confession is healing—all rolled in one. Confession is what souls are crying for. Will you tend to that cry?

I know the Sacrament of Reconciliation can seem scary at first, but it's really not; it's freeing. My son recently showed me a bird's nest and was poking at it with the end of a broom handle. I told him not to do that, and I went back inside the house. He said he wanted to knock it down, but I told him not to because I could see the top of a little bird's head. About five minutes later, he came to the back door upset that he hadn't believed me. He knocked the nest down anyway, and there were three birds on the ground. I went with him to the nest and saw the awful sight. His dad came over and put them back in the nest and put the nest back up. I don't think the mom came back for them.

My son told me, "Mama, I have that thing

in me from what I did. I want to go to the priest."

I said, "You mean reconciliation, confession?" He said "Yes!" He asked me about it a second time. What he'd done to those little baby birds was really bothering him, thank God. We went the following Saturday and stood in line and confessed our sins.

I told a family member this story, and she said, "Oh, you think you can just go to confession, and that makes what he did OK."

I said nothing, but my thought was, "You are such a wounded soul. You need confession and to experience the love and mercy of God to be able to understand." It's so hard to see what I see, and yet I can't convince people—that is not so easy. It must be so hard, sad, and frustrating for all of heaven. As Father Jerry said, "God must be so frustrated, since the beginning of time He has been trying to prove to man that we are happier with Him in our lives."

Teach your children by example what healing there is in being absolved of your sins. There is light in breaking down the wall between you and Jesus. It's easy for time to fly by; sometimes when I don't feel as close to Jesus, it will remind me to stop and think just how long it's been since I confessed my sins. Even though I don't commit the same sins I used to, the Lord is working on me to grow all the time, and the way to do that is to reveal things that I need to improve on or change about myself. It would be too much to do it all at once, so it is a slow and continuous process of weeding out the dark and bringing in more light. I wonder what He will help me with next. It's usually something I am oblivious to. That's the point; that's why I need Him, always and forever. If you have ever gardened or trimmed bushes, you've probably noticed how the new, beautiful growth comes out the following year. It's the same with us. It's the only way we can grow—to cut the dead parts off. The dead parts are our sins, which cause us pain.

Nine

THE ADDICTION

"Behold, I will treat and assuage
the city's wounds; I will heal them
and reveal to them an abundance
of lasting peace."

Jeremiah 33:6

For so long I thought it was normal that I masturbated nearly every day, just as I thought it was normal that I thought about sex all the time.

When I was a teenager, my dad would say, "If we cut open your head, a bunch of boys would run out."

I thought, "How does he know that?" I thought it was normal that I fantasized all the time. Fantasy was an escape from my reality of being empty, full of shame, and lonely. I would escape and imagine different love sessions of intimacy. What a joke—that isn't intimacy. I was afraid of intimacy. I didn't need any porn. There were mushy romance novels in my head, almost like plays or movies. This would happen especially when I was bored or tired or lonely, although at the time I didn't realize when or why it happened. During recovery, I learned it is called HALTS: hungry, angry, lonely, tired, or stressed. Addicts have a hard time with self-care. The treatment I received in June of 2012 was life changing to me, for the better.

Most of my friends and family didn't think I

was an addict. Of course, I didn't either. I knew I felt bad after I had sex with men when I was dating them, but I didn't really understand why. It seemed I couldn't wait longer than three weeks or so. If I drank too much on a date, then sometimes I didn't even wait that long. I would have sex too soon into a relationship or before one was even established. To feel better about it, I would throw all of myself into trying to have a relationship with the person to justify that it was OK that I had sex with him. Sometimes I really liked the person, but sometimes I think I just tried to like him to recover so that I didn't feel so bad about having sex with him.

After Charles and I had sex, I finally made that call to a counselor who specialized in sex addiction. I told him about my previous counselor, whom I had stopped seeing in January, and who said "you can be addicted to people"; I told him how I had learned about love and sex addiction.

He said, "Dawn, you are a sex addict. It is hard for women to admit to that."

We are supposed to be virginal. When a guy you are dating and having sex with asks how many people you have had sex with, and you start out by dividing by two to bring the number down, and then you get up to dividing by seven, that is not a good thing. The divisor keeps getting higher.

It was hard for me to believe I was a sex addict, but deep down I knew the counselor was right. I didn't have sex with strangers, but what's the definition of a stranger? I wasn't into porn. I have watched it when I dated a guy who liked to watch it, but it disgusted me. It looked like the girls were being hurt. I couldn't understand why it would be a turn-on.

I thought I was just looking for love like Carrie Bradshaw in *Sex and the City*. But unlike Carrie, I didn't have a guy who I dated on and off again and couldn't get over for ten years—a guy with a limo, a guy who would one day marry me. I wasn't like Samantha, either, the character who would run into the Fed Ex guy as he delivered a package to her office, have sex with him, and then not want to see him again. In my twenties, I did have what would be called a one-night stand, when I went out with friends, drank too much, and woke up with some guy. Then I felt bad and hoped he would want to see me again, even if I didn't really like him. I had to justify the behavior as OK. It was just drinking too much, having a fun time with my friends. "Just drinking too much." Some girls have gotten killed that way, like Natalie Holloway. That could have happened to me or any one of my friends. Alcohol was the catalyst for my destructive behavior.

We lived in a young party town at the time and could walk to the bars. The guys we met lived there too, and it seemed harmless. I think there was some blacking out there, since at times I wouldn't remember the hooking-up part. I gave myself away, not even remembering anything. I felt bad about it, but I thought it was justified since my friends were doing it also. It didn't seem so bad; it just seemed like sewing my wild twenty-something oats. It's in many television shows and movies, but there never is a caption: "Warning, don't try this at home, as it could lead to a broken spirit." The world is in the dark.

In *Sex in the City*, they were doing the same thing as my friends and I were. That's one reason the show was such a big hit; most could identify with the characters. They talked and laughed about the same things we had issues with. It all seemed so normal. Yet, it was getting harder to look at myself in the mirror. I remember one of my close friends got close to God around the time I had gotten pregnant. She wouldn't come to my wedding because she didn't support my reason for getting married—because I was pregnant. That hurt, and I didn't understand. I thought, "A year ago, you were smoking cigarettes, drinking, and having sex right along with me. We were nearly each other's wing man, so what happened?" God happened, and

He was showing her a path to the light. She had warned me about watching shows like *Sex in the City*. I wasn't ready to hear it. I see how it can be hard to meet people where they are on their journey. You forget where you started from, and then you can end up pushing them away from God.

Secular seems normal because everyone is doing it. Yet, it is horrible to our souls; we do feel bad because God doesn't want us to live this way. Not because He is no fun, but because nothing good comes from it. It only leads us down a darker path. The behavior becomes normal and is repeated over and over again. Is it a habit or an addiction? Habits can be broken—never easily though. Mark Twain said, "Habit is habit, and not to be flung out the window by any man, but coaxed downstairs one step at a time." Addictions are another issue, as you can tell from my story. To feel better, we may do other things to medicate and cope with our addiction. For me, it was being a neat freak, as in cleaning everything and organizing everything.

Can we change what this world views as normal? When I told a guy my story and that I would only wait three weeks before I had sex, his reply was, "That is a long time for our age group." I was like, really? If we aren't part of the solution, then we very well could be part of the problem. The way I lived,

I really didn't need anyone to tell me it was wrong, for my very soul felt it—as I think so many others do too, when they don't live in accordance with God.

When my dad would tell me not to have sex on a date because no man would want to marry me, I rebelled. He would say, "If you give away the milk, nobody will want to buy the cow."

I got fed up with this statement from him sometime during my twenties and told him, "I want some milk for myself, and my cow isn't for sale." It fueled my ambition to prove that I could have sex like a man, which to me meant without feelings and without becoming attached. I also viewed it as having sex just for the pleasure of it, but as much as I wanted to be wired that way, my heart and soul were not. My darkness and pain increased with each partner, and I knew something was wrong with me, but I didn't know what it was. I never imagined—ever—that I was an addict. I pictured addicts as people who couldn't go to work because their addiction overpowered them, keeping them from doing the things they needed to accomplish in a day. It wasn't like that for me. Maybe addiction for those of us who believe in God could be: what do you put before God? If you can stop, then it's probably just a habit. If you can't, then it could be an addiction. I think most of us never try to find out.

At my first visit to my counselor for sex addiction treatment, he advised me to fill out a questionnaire online. I spent $250 dollars to see if I was a sex addict, and I still didn't believe it. My counselor already knew I was one by what I had filled him in on, but I thought the results would say that I wasn't one. The result would give him insight as to how severe my addiction was. I didn't have sex with animals or hire prostitutes or seek opportunities to have sex. Some of the questions on the questionnaire were quite disgusting. I guess the masturbation and the conversation geared toward sex, and then of course the partners I've had when I was between the ages of fifteen and thirty-eight, all pointed to it. It didn't seem too bad at the time. Time catches up with us, though. I did have some relationships that lasted two or three years. Some years I had sex with multiple partners. Looking back, those were years I was lonely or rebounding from a broken relationship, not realizing it was called depression. I had nothing to compare it to, so I thought it was normal. I had always dealt with anxiety, and I thought that was normal too.

I was forever thinking I had met my prince charming, and then he always seemed to turn into a frog. The day and age we live in features songs about sex and having sex and looking sexy, and in most of the television shows and the movies there is sexual content. I just thought I was normal.

When I told my girlfriend from college about my book and the topic, her response was, "You will probably be famous one day."

I said, "I hope not."

She said, "We have all been there and done that, but nobody has the courage to talk about it."

In our world and circle and extended circle of friends, it is normal. Just how far does the circle extend out to? It's not normal for everyone. Yet, does anyone know the word "chastity" anymore, or the definition of it? I have two friends who had sex with one person before marriage and they married that person. That amazes me—or it used to. I couldn't imagine what that would be like. How did they only sleep with one person their entire lives? I know that must sound sad to some, but, sadly, others can relate.

Another friend told me she played a truth-or-dare game at a bar, and that question came up—how many people she had slept with—and she said "one." She didn't consider oral sex in the rankings with vaginal sex. I never used to either. She was a "I-will-do-everything-but-vaginal-sex" girl. They looked at her then-boyfriend, who is now her husband, and they were amazed. She said she remembered feeling so proud of herself since everyone was so amazed, and she knew why.

My other friend said she wanted to test out what she was marrying. Why? Because if he was no good in bed, she wouldn't have married him? Yet, the old me, would have agreed with all of their justifications. It would have made sense to me; now it doesn't, but now I love God. Even the not-so-obvious sinner has justifications. The evil guy does it to us all. To live a chaste life in our culture isn't something we strive to teach our youth. Parents pray their kids won't get pregnant before they are married. We have forgotten to teach them to love God above everything, if we even teach our children to love God at all. Remember, children learn best by watching our lives. We don't think about their souls because we don't think about our own. We just think about what kind of college they will go to and what type of grades they need to get into those colleges. What sports are they playing, and what activities are they in? That's the most common question I'm asked: "What does your son do?"

Sadly, in our culture, it's more normal to have several sexual partners than one for your entire life. At sixteen, I didn't know that my behavior was leading me down a dark road to addiction. My other friend who has only had sex with one person—

her husband—told me it was embarrassing not to be promiscuous. She said when people talked of such things, she just never said anything so that they could think what they wanted to. That's pretty sad when it's not cool to have morals and values.

I asked her, "Did your dad listen to you and value your opinion and spend his time with you?"

She said, "Oh yes, my dad had me up here," as she raised her arm up. "He thought I was all that."

Wow, could we have her dad teach other dads that? Many would be sad that the promiscuous girls with daddy issues would go extinct. Men would actually have to wait until marriage to have sex, and they would have to learn to treat women with respect, dignity, and love. I wonder what role the mom plays with the boys, teaching them how to treat women. What am I doing wrong as a mom? Do you see how we don't learn the important things in school, the things that make our society and culture what it could be for the better? We are supposed to learn it at home. We learn how to be an addict at home.

I have a friend Laura who is fifty-five and on her third marriage with a similar story to mine. She used to meet men in hotel rooms—men she'd met on the Internet. She used to call me afterward, upset, and I could tell she had been drinking. Her monster was bigger than mine. I might have gotten to that point if I hadn't wanted my serpent dead and been willing to do the work to kill it. Laura has since been to confession at the Solanus Casey Center, and she's on the road to healing. She doesn't meet men in hotel rooms or have affairs with men she meets through work anymore. She has a lot of work to do, but she is aware. She thanked me when I told her my story, because then she told me hers. We disappointed the serpent. He wants us to live in darkness, alone with our afflictions. For when we tell another, it sheds light and starves the beast. Laura can see that her daughters have similar love and sex addiction issues to hers. She has not told them about her issues yet. I keep encouraging her to do so since they are in their twenties now. It is scary and embarrassing to share our skeletons with our children, but if we don't, we are not giving them much more of a chance to heal than we had. It's not fair to them. It's risky to tell them because we can't predict their reaction, but it is out of love for them to be able to conquer their own darkness. All three of Laura's children have gotten pregnant before marriage. One day, Jesus is coming back, and they or their children might not have as long to battle the darkness as we did. We have to give them a fighting chance to get to heaven. I would rather spend all eternity with my son and have him disappointed in me on Earth than have the other alternative because he didn't have enough time on Earth to come to Jesus due to the family tradition of darkness.

When I tell guys that I am a sex addict, they say, "Oh, I wish I had known you before you recovered." Or they say something like, "I like sex too." I am telling them my story to shed light on their darkness, but they don't seem to get it. No offense to any man reading this, but if you can see your darkness, I give you lots of credit for that. I think it's harder for men to see sex as an addiction—or any darkness for that matter. My counselor said most men only come in for sex addiction treatment when they have been caught by the law or their spouse. Every woman I told my story to from ages seventeen to sixty-seven told me her version of her story—maybe not always admitting that she was a sex addict, for maybe she just didn't know or maybe it was a habit. At least I saw a light bulb go on while she would reveal to me something that bothered her about how she lived her life in her relationships with men.

I have a favorite quote by Bishop Fulton Sheen:

"When a man loves a woman, he has to become worthy of her. The higher her virtue, the more noble her character, and the more devoted she is to truth, justice, goodness, the more a man has to aspire to be worthy of her.

The history of civilization could actually be written in terms of the level of its women."

Are you ready, girls, to change the world? Let's help each other and get healthy and bring back to the world just how special we are. Let's remind each other that we carry life and are the givers of life, not the destroyers of life. Let us stop competing with each other for a man who just wants to take something from us. Let us join forces and unite to be the makers of history. Together we can bring back respect, dignity, and virtue for ourselves. *We can be the healers of this world. God's love through us is enough to heal the world.*

Since I was a teenager, my thoughts were mostly about sex. The words I spoke and the jokes I made held many references to sex. My actions were very sexual. I could see it in the way I dressed at times, the flirting and the masturbation. It became a habit. It became the center of my life, and without realizing it, looking back, it was my character. It kept me from the life I wanted. For so long I was unhappy, but I didn't know sex was the reason why. I thought sex was what made me happy. I didn't know I had to change my thought patterns. I didn't know I could. I certainly didn't know it would make me happy. Wow! I can live without sex and be full of joy! Sex was keeping me from my joy. It wasn't giving me joy like I thought it would. It was giving me moments of pleasure followed by much sadness and depression. A few minutes of pleasure didn't last long. I was constantly empty. It is one of the worst feelings in the world. You never really put your finger on it—why or how to fill it. When you become aware, you realize that you shop, gamble, watch television, play sports, work, eat, exercise, read, have sex, or drink too much. But the emptiness comes back. I know a secret! I know how to fill up the emptiness. Realize that God loves you. I mean really get it. Accept His love and forgiveness for your past—whatever your past is or isn't. God's love can help you with any and every part of your life. I think counseling does help you to become aware, if you find the right psychologist or counselor. When you have had enough of trying to be in control of your life, remember: God heals. God directs us to those who can help us. I know He did for me. He can for you too; it starts by spending time with Him. Call out, "Jesus, please help me," and never stop calling His name for help until He sends the angels for you to bring you home.

The books *The Return of the Prodigal Son,* by Henri Nouwen, and *Abba's Child*, by Brennan Manning, both had a huge part in bringing me to accept God's love and forgiveness. That is the hard part—realizing how much God loves you, and that He has sent His Son to heal and forgive you, and that Jesus will bring you to Him. I realized how much heaven loves me and wants me to return home to them, and that they are waiting for us all to return home. It made me fall in love with God. I fell in love with Jesus, and I now love Him more than anything. That is what it takes to get better. You fall in love with Jesus and surrender the rest to Him.

"Do you not know that your body is a temple of the Holy Spirit within you, whom you have from God, and that you are not your own? For you have been purchased at a price. Therefore glorify God in your body" (1 Corinthians 6:19–20).

In June of 2012, I went to Arizona for a week at an outpatient rehab center. It included fifty hours of counseling, ten hours a day. There were twenty hours of group counseling and thirty hours of private counseling. In my life, I never had a lasting relationship. I was never happy. I was overly critical of myself and others. I attracted nearly the same person over and over again and was expecting a different result. I was overlooking the fact that I was the common denominator in all of my relationships. I went there to change that.

For years I blamed the men. Oh, they were all jerks—that's what I thought. Controlling jerks. But what was I? In my own way, I was a controlling person. When we judge others, whatever we are judging them about, it says something about us. Is it a reflection of how we feel about ourselves, or is it a truth we don't want to admit about ourselves? When you are criticized or judged by someone, try to discern if it is really about you. Look for the truth in it and be honest with yourself. Some of the time, though, it will tell you about the person doing the criticizing. Things they are not even mindfully aware of about themselves. Some are so sensitive to criticism. It is because they are so wounded. Usually the people most sensitive to criticism are the ones who are overly critical toward others. They cause others pain. They probably had parents or caregivers who were overly critical of them. It is like their nerves are raw, and even though they dish it out the most, they can't take it in return. So don't bother; it is like waking a hungry lion. Do what Jesus says and turn the other cheek. When we spend time with God and pray and meditate, we can stay centered and see reality more clearly. We stop taking everything so personally. We can then see another's pain.

When the counselors suggested I call my parents from rehab to tell them how I felt, I dragged my feet. My problem was that I felt responsible for another's feelings. They were trying to get through to me that how I felt mattered too. I called my mom to set up a time when she and my dad would be home, but my mom still didn't think I was a sex addict, even though I had told her about my past and why I was going. She told me my father didn't know why I was in Arizona. He thought I was there for work.

I said, "Mom, for me to get better, they want to have a conference call with you, dad, the therapist, and me." I was very hesitant about this. They told me on Wednesday midday that I needed to call my parents and tell them how I felt. I said I couldn't do that because it would hurt their feelings. That is why I was a "stuffer." I never wanted to hurt anyone's feelings. I didn't feel that what I wanted or felt mattered more than what someone else wanted or felt, especially my parents.

They said, "Dawn, calling your parents is like slaying the dragon. You have to do this to get better. If you can tell them how you feel, then you will be able to tell others how you feel."

I couldn't hide from others and bury what caused me pain anymore, even from my parents. I had to address the issue. It started with those closest to me. The rest of the day Wednesday I felt sick and was adamant that I couldn't call them. I just couldn't do that to them. It would be so hurtful. They gave me such a good childhood. I had braces, a six-week trip to Europe at age fourteen to see my pen pal, and a car at sixteen; they even paid for my college education. We spent the summers at our lake house and spent the winter's snowmobiling and exploring the northern and eastern sides of Michigan's snowmobile trails. My dad always told me not to worry about money—that he was my bank. I am where I am financially because of his help. Yet, the counselor's saying it was the only way I would get better rang in my ears like a broken record. I realized I had come too far and spent too much money to stop now. I had to do the hardest thing I ever had to do in my entire life. I had to tell my parents something negative about how I felt about them.

They teach you to say a positive with it. You are supposed to say the word "and" in between, with the positive statement going first. I messed up and said the word "but." The word "but" erases the positive. At the time, the phone call went great. I had this idea built up in my head that my dad was a villain and my mom was a saint. They wanted to break me of this—to not see the world as all good or all bad or black and white.

I told my dad that I had many relationships and I wanted to stop living my life this way, so I was getting help for my sex addiction. He said he could understand that.

My mom said on the phone to the therapist and me, "Dawn, you aren't a sex addict, you are just promiscuous."

The therapist kind of chuckled at that one as she looked at me. My mom got married at sixteen and my dad at nineteen, and they were both virgins. Maybe they had a love addiction, but they definitely weren't out sleeping around with other people. Maybe our culture helped to create the monster in me with the clothes, music, and movies—well, I know it didn't help things.

My mom said she didn't like sex until well into the marriage when she had a neighbor lady have a talk with her about it. She said that is why she didn't think she had to talk to us girls about it. She didn't like it so she thought we wouldn't either. She never thought it would become the problem that it became for me. It's important to talk to teenagers about sex—not just telling them to stay pure and "just say no." We need to educate them about sex addiction. If they are heading down a road, they need the knowledge that it is OK to get help and that there is help out there. We need to educate our young people about addiction so they have the power of that knowledge. We need to not treat addicts like the lepers of long ago. Let's get it out there and talk about it and come out of the closet on this. It's our only fighting chance against it. We need to heal our wounded souls in the world instead of looking at them as a lost cause. We need to educate our young people about the wounds that possibly lie hidden deep within. It is the healing of these wounds that will be the bridge to a life free of deadly sin.

I went on in a quivering voice to my dad that I thought he was a great provider and he took very good care of me financially, but that his anger and rage at me at times were unwarranted. He didn't need to be so severe, especially to a little girl.

He said, "Yes, I think at times I was stressed out and probably took it out on you a little too much." I was shocked that he sounded so compassionate and understanding.

The one that did him in was what I said to my mom. I said, "Mom, I think you were a great mom and always there for me at home, but you didn't protect me from his anger." I can't remember what anyone said after that.

A few weeks after I came home and I was up at their house, my mom said to me, "I couldn't have told my mother what you told me."

I said nothing.

Later that weekend, I was helping my dad

get ready for a car show at his home. We had been working all day, and he looked at me with his piercing eyes and said, "She didn't protect you from me." He said it out of the blue. I got the message that what I told them did hurt him, or that what I told my mom hurt her so much that it hurt him as well.

They since have forgiven me. My dad may never be the nurturing, unconditional-love kind of dad. He is my dad, and I forgive him; after all, he is wounded too.

My parents couldn't see that I just wanted to get better. I just wanted to stand up for myself and tell people in my life how I felt. I wanted to tell the men in my life when I felt they were being mean or wrong or hurtful to me instead of keeping it in until I exploded and ended the relationship. The kind of guys I attracted—well, I don't think they liked a girl with a voice. I think if I would have had a voice all along, a lot of my adult wounds wouldn't have happened. I wouldn't have gotten involved with men who treated me like an object for meeting their needs. I would have been healthy enough to not treat them as objects either. I would have had to see them not as what they could give me, which was *love*—that four-letter word that I was forever seeking, never really knowing how to give what it meant. I only knew how to give sex and be what I thought men wanted me to be, without it ever really being intimacy. Sex isn't intimacy, but the dark spirit had me fooled into believing that it was. He wanted my soul for all eternity.

Thank God my Lord is stronger than him. My Lord died for me so I don't have to carry the stains of my sins with me. My Lord is a Healer, and He healed me. He bound up all my wounds. He made me brand-new. God renewed my soul into someone who can love and be loved and into someone who can forgive and be forgiven. If I would have loved myself, I never would have treated my body like an object to be used. I never would have treated my body like a tool to get what I wanted, which was love. God helped me to realize that I am one of His beloved daughters. That is who I am. I am not a sex addict. I *was* a sex addict. I was a lost soul looking for love through sex with any guy who gave me attention. The men who gave me attention were also lost souls and looking for something. Water seeks its own level.

For some reason, most of my life I felt ugly. I realize now it wasn't about my looks, it was that my soul was ugly. I was feeling the ugliness of my soul and projecting it onto how I felt about myself physically. There was a movie called *Swingers* that was popular when I was twenty-five. In the movie, the guy called girls "pretty babies." I remember my boyfriend at the time, Donnie, looking at me and saying, "You're a pretty baby, aren't you?" I got the feeling that he didn't think I was pretty enough for him, so he was trying to convince both of us that I was. He was really cute, and nope, I didn't feel pretty enough for him. I tried to make up for it in other ways. I thought by being skinny and working out and watching what I ate—maybe a little too much—would help keep Donnie attracted to me. I wore tight, sexy clothes and was ready to have sex whenever he wanted, even if I didn't feel good. I used to blame guys like Donnie, but I take the responsibility. I hated myself and I felt ugly, never realizing there was something deeply wrong inside. I searched for my soul mate until my soul broke. I didn't want to do it anymore. But I couldn't stop.

Masturbation kept me isolated. I was proud of the fact that I didn't "need" a man and that I could take care of "my own chores." I didn't realize that I could stop masturbating, and that I needed to, until I entered a twelve-step program for Sexaholics Anonymous. It was a support group to help me keep from having sex with myself or any person outside of marriage. The group helped me to learn so much. I learned things that I didn't learn in rehab or through my counseling sessions, as there is so much to be learned about this disease of addiction. Mostly I didn't feel alone; there were other people out there like me, struggling with the same things that I struggled with. Our stories were all different, and even our behaviors differed too. We had a common theme—we were in pain. I didn't look at them as bad people. It helped me to stop looking at myself as a bad person unworthy of love.

One of the Jewish guys in his early twenties spoke of how his rabbi was helping him with his pornography addiction. He explained how he had to keep his computer locked from himself and have his brother hold the password and keep changing it. He couldn't be alone with his computer. He spoke of how it started while he was home alone when his parents were at work as a young teen. Most of the guys told him how awesome it was that he was addressing this and taking care of it at such a young age. The longer you leave the serpent alone with you, the more he grows. He gets his power in our isolation and secretiveness. As our society moves farther away from God and the spiritual life, it makes sense that mental health in our society is decreasing. Without God we have the serpent, and with the serpent we have mental sickness. The more God gets pushed out, the more mentally sick this country is going to get.

The week I spent in rehab changed my life. They saw things I didn't see. They told me what I needed to do to get better. I had to tell people what I was feeling about them, the people that mattered most in my life. They taught me it was OK to have a voice and to have an opinion, and that I mattered and it mattered how I felt about something. I now allow myself to speak and not bury it when something or someone makes me sad or angry. I have to get it out, and I have the courage to do so. When we bury, we stuff. When we stuff, we have to use something to stuff it down with to deal with it. What is your stuffer of choice? To stuff means to not deal with things that upset us, to ignore them or to medicate with something until a later time. Mine were men and masturbation. I loved to live in my head in the fantasy world of having sex. I thought there was nothing wrong with it. It didn't hurt anyone, not even me—that's what I thought. I had so many failed relationships. I seemed to pick the same person over and over again. Usually I felt scared of these men. Even certain women intimidated me. I lived in a world of black and white. Either people were good or bad, nice or mean. There was no "in between" for me. You were an awesome person until you did something to hurt me. Well you could hurt me ten or twenty times. I was never sure when the straw would break the camel's back, and then suddenly I would go the other extreme of hating you. I would have stuffed all those times from one to nineteen. On number twenty, you would have gotten the brunt of all the feelings from the other nineteen times along with number twenty. So you wouldn't understand. I would explode.

I had to learn that you tell someone how you feel at incident number two, number seventeen, and everything in between. Then it comes out pretty calm. I only knew anger as explosive anger. Rage— I remember rage from when I was a child. I had turned into my father during those raging times.

I remember yelling at my son, and he looked so scared. I thought, "I have to stop. I am doing the same thing to him that my dad did to me." I said to him, "Tell me how you felt when I was yelling at you."

He said, "I was scared, and it's not OK." He took his Lego creation and smashed it up against the table to show me what he thought I was going to do to him.

He is right; it's not OK. I don't wait too long to discipline him now. I work on doing it sooner when my anger level is at a two, not at a nine when I am explosive. I can have compassion for my father now. Someone was like that to him. I refuse to carry on the family tradition. We teach our children how to treat their children. By how we treat our children, we teach them how to treat others and how someone can treat them as adults.

"Now to him who is able to accomplish far more than all we ask or imagine, by the power at work within us, to him be glory in the church and in Christ Jesus to all generations, forever and ever. Amen"

Ephesians 3:20

Ten

TEMPTATION

"Behold, I am sending you like sheep in the midst of wolves; so be shrewd as serpents and simple as doves."

Matthew 10:16

The summer following rehab, there was a married guy who was a bit too talkative to me, and I let him know. He said that his wife had a friend who was a man, and they even went to lunch or dinner sometimes, and that we should do that. I said it was fine that he was OK with that, but that I was not comfortable with that. I always had a hard time before with saying no and hurting someone's feelings. This time, at least, I recognized that, yes, I have a hard time with it, but I need to fight through it. I told him about my addiction, my treatment and week in rehab, and the year and a half of counseling and the twelve step program. I thought that it would help him. Maybe he would realize that he possibly had some sex addiction issues, since, in time, he flat out told me he wanted to have sex with me. I told him it was wrong for us to even be talking. We were heading down a path of which nothing good would come. The fact that I told him about my addiction issues only made things worse. He only came after me more. I thought he would respect my wishes more and have compassion for my struggles. I suppose that is where I was naïve: to think that the type of men I attracted would be respectful of what I thought. They don't ever seem to care what I want. When I do have a voice, they still don't want to listen to it or respect it. The only thing to do was to learn to get really strong boundaries, and to keep those boundaries and guard them, for it was my soul at risk.

There always will be temptation; the serpent can assure us of that one. Know your weakness and it will help identify when you are being tempted. Temptation stems from the seeds of evil; if seeds are planted, it can lead to sin and become your root of evil of the darkness that we are unaware of that lies within.

I had come so far in my treatment and worked so hard to get healthy, I could not let this guy take me down back the path to the dark pit of hell. It wasn't easy. It did fire up my addict, and she started driving the bus again. I hated myself for being attracted to him. It disgusted me to think this was a representative of who I attracted and who I gave myself away to all of those times. This was the first married person, but it seemed the serpent was upping the stakes. He wanted to try to take me down and take me down hard. The serpent knew if I'd had sex with that married man, how horrible I would have felt, he wants us to hate ourselves. Once I was not in my lustful state, I was not attracted to the married guy anyway. He was fifteen years older than me. I thought he was so smart and successful, and to me, that exuded power. The addict part of me wants to overtake that power to feel powerful herself. I never saw that either, all those years.

I am thankful for my church family. My small Catholic2Catholic group at my church prayed over me, and prayer is powerful. Could this be the new normal, praying over people? As in giving people a bit of heaven, through the laying on of hands just like the book of Acts. The big thing was that I told them. It is scary to tell anyone, "Hey, this married guy is after me." Empathy and mercy are so needed today; it is what this world lacks most besides unconditional love. I needed help to continue to say no and to keep my boundaries strong. I needed to realize that nobody deserves to take away my freedom and to take away my power, and that I am not the victim. I will not play the part of the victim anymore. I am a beloved daughter of God, and I am strong. "I have the strength for everything through him who empowers me." (Philippians 4:13)

Strengthen me is just what He did. The serpent wanted me so he sent a wolf out to take me, but my God is stronger than the serpent. Thank you, Lord, I am set free! I realize that guy is a wounded soul. I also realize I can't save him. It did no good to tell him my story. It only gave him more power over me. He said, "I like sex too," after I told him about my struggles. That is the irony. I have found I don't miss sex. I have found I must not have liked it as much as I thought I did. There was a sickness there that I needed healing. How many others are out there with varying shades and degrees of this sickness? It seems like so many, now that I can see mine. I cry for them, and I pray by the grace of God that they come into His eternal light and have the courage to get help to stop. I am sure sex can be beautiful when you are married and you love each other in a healthy way. The way I experienced sex in my life made it dark and dirty and disgusting.

I had a guy tell me he is not attracted to his wife any longer because she has gained weight. As a result, he stated he didn't want to have sex with her. The same issue happened with his first wife. I think there needs to be some major healing there. I don't think unconditional love looks at weight to that degree. Maybe he suffers from sexual anorexia. Anorexia means interrupted appetite. People who have sexual anorexia avoid, fear, or dread sexual intimacy." Seeking out a new partner doesn't help matters. I asked him if he had a new spouse he was attracted to just how long would it be before he had the same problem. He is the common denominator in both relationships, just as I was the one in all of my failed relationships. My girlfriend told me her husband put a lot of pressure on her to be thin, and she ended up with bulimia. Sex addicts objectify and turn the bodies of God's children into objects instead of looking at someone as having feelings, wounds, and pain.

I often think of my friend whose husband doesn't want to have sex with her and yet watches porn on the Internet. He is throwing so much away. The biggest problem with addiction is the denial. The enemy is at the core of an addiction. It's the easiest way for him to get our souls. It is such a slow and painful death. Maybe having us not believe or remember that he exists is the easiest way to ruin lives and souls. In that area, he seems to have multitudes and multitudes of people right where he wants him. I know he used to have me.

I think about the man who goes about stopping at different women's desks at work in need of attention. He can't get a boob job and wear a tight skirt like women do to get attention. He goes about it in a different way. He intrudes on people's lives; he's unwelcome, but to him, he is just being social. Why are the fluttering visits only to females then? Why do the e mailed jokes only have women on the distribution list? He is missing out on life like I was but in a different way, using all his energy on shallow relationships; when the girls see him coming, they want to go the other way. He is looked at as a lonely guy, but there is more to it than that. If it was just that, he would make some guy friends to hang out with.

> "This illness is not to end in death, but is for the glory of God, that the Son of God may be glorified through it." (John 11:4)

The fact that you see the world as you see it, not as it really is, doesn't help your denial. Even though everywhere we turn, our oversexualized culture supports casual sex, it won't protect you from the damage it does to your soul. Ralph Waldo Emerson said, "The most dangerous thing is illusion." Whether you call it an addiction or just a habit, it is this thing called "sex for fun." Sex for your own selfish pleasure can eventually ruin your life. Most won't see it as this. Some may, and others may just have a seed planted that hopefully one day buds. Telling my humiliating story will be worth it if just one person's soul is saved from further self-destruction. It is so important to love God, forgive yourself, and forgive others. Live mindfully aware that the choices we make affect our growth and well-being.

When I think of God and His light, the words that come to mind are: compassion, mercy, love, selflessness, self-knowledge, truth, enlightenment, healing, benevolence, a good disposition, and the drive to help and serve others. When I think of Satan and darkness, the words that come to mind are: hatred, aggression, malevolence, wrath, sloth, avarice, lust, pride, gluttony, and envy. Because we are born into original sin, we encompass both good and evil. God gives us free will. We think we don't need a savior because we don't realize at all what is going on within our heads. The health of your brain determines your behavior, which determines the color of your soul. Our behavior shows we are sick. We can't go by what is normal and acceptable to society. The society in which we live is sick. You have to be mindful of that. Living a life not mindful of what you are doing or why you are doing it is death. It will lead to the death of your soul.

Eleven

REFLECTING

"God is our refuge and our strength, an ever present help in distress. Thus we do not fear, though earth be shaken and mountains quake to the depths of the sea, though its waters rage and foam and mountains totter at its surging. The Lord of hosts is with us."

Psalm 46:2-4

Looking back, I can't believe I lived this way for so long. I cried often and was depressed much of the time. I had nothing to compare it to. Nobody talks about this stuff. We hide it, even from ourselves. Anxiety and depression are huge symptoms of addiction. I didn't know any other way to feel so I thought it was normal, but what is normal?

I had to fill out a form at rehab to rate my anxiety and depression. I rated it on the low side, and my counselor said, "Dawn, this doesn't look like a sick person to me."

I said, "Well, what do I have to compare it to?"

He said, "That's true."

I was told at rehab I either tended to minimize things or overreact to things. I could see that but not until they brought it to my attention. I usually minimized things. Many people are on a happy pill to deal with life; they don't know they need to face their pain, or they refuse to do so. They don't even know they have it, or if they do, that they can do something about it. They think this is the way life is, and they watch porn, drink every night, or shop when they can't

afford it. It is their normal; it is all they know.

As kids, and in our teens and twenties, our friends mean so much to us at that time in our lives. I think of my best friend I had from preschool to about the fifth grade and how controlling she was of me. Looking back, it was a huge indicator of how my life was going to go. I wonder, if I would have stood up to that girl so long ago, would my life have been different? I was a doormat even then. I was scared of her, literally. Typical of how my adult relationships went, I could only take so much from her and then I would blow up. Her mom got on the phone once and said, "You can call back when you cool off." I see it with my son and his friends. He has a couple stronger friends that come around, and I try to make him aware of what is going on and for him to stand up to them. Yet, there is one boy who reminds me of me when I was little. I feel so bad for that boy. I tell my son not to be so bossy with him. My son has a strong personality, yet there are kids stronger than him. I see those kids as more wounded than my son, but then I think of the doormat friend of his. We are all wounded. We all have pain. We are all in need of healing.

Sometimes the friends are bad influences, but the companionship that comes from sharing the pain helps soothe the soul even as it darkens it. As we get older, people start to break away. They get married or get busy with work and their own lives. People don't see or call each other as much. When you do talk to catch up with an old friend, it's more superficial talk. Are you really going to be real? I mean, you can't even get real with yourself. So time goes on, and you get into your thirties and you realize things. Maybe you start to go after your dreams or change them or give up on some. You really end up growing up in your thirties. You realize it is not turning out the way you thought it would. Either you get more controlling, or you learn to give up some of the control. You start down a path of further self-destruction, or you realize you are a work in progress and try to make adjustments along the way. It may happen sooner for some or later for others. Experience only tells that tale, and the journey is different for everyone. Many that divorce stay stuck, going through the motions of life. As single parents, we don't have much time; nobody has enough time. We work and buy things and work on the things we buy. We get used to our lonely lives, and it becomes a routine.

You are living a life that God didn't create you to live. You are lied to by the father of lies, and you think you have no choice, and that this is your fate. You are accepted in society for the most part as normal, at least by a good percentage. What is the pain of living that way? For I know it is a wound, whether inherited through mental illness, or created from childhood, or both. If you spent time with the Lord and received healing, you could stop. Do you love the Lord more than anything in your life? Do you want your serpent dead? It's not just the addicts that put things before God to escape from life. This life is a painful life; we aren't meant for this world. The Blessed Virgin Mary told St. Bernadette the first time she spoke to her, "I cannot promise you happiness in this life, only in the next." To not feel is to not live in reality. To not live in reality is to escape. To stay mindful of our thoughts and to feel is too much for us. It is why everyone needs a savior. We are all in need of saving from the darkness that tries to get in. As Bishop Byrnes said, "No one is immune from it, nobody."

I finally realized that for my pain to end, I needed help from counseling and from God. The counseling made me aware of things I was doing, patterns that I didn't even see, which still amazes me. For example, at rehab they told me I like to have men over and play house, have drinks, make them dinner, and then have sex with them.

They said, "You want them on your territory, and you want the control."

I said, "What, me?" I mean, yes, I like to entertain and hang at my house, but it's a pattern and a bad one?

They said it was a red light behavior for me. They told me not to have men over and not to drink on a date.

I thought, but that is so much fun—correction, that *was* so much fun. The pain was greater than the good time. That is when you know you are ready to admit to what they are saying and be thankful to turn the other way. That is an example of why counseling was great. I was living my life with blinders on. My mask was so thick it was one with my soul. It was destroying me, and I didn't even know it. I was on a dark path, and I had been on it so long. I couldn't see any light. My eyes had adjusted to the darkness! I thought I could see where I was going. If I could have, I never would have kept on that road. Or maybe the problem is that we see nothing wrong with the road we are on.

God gave me the healing I needed, healing that only He could give. He killed the serpent. The evil guy tries to jump back on, but once he is off and you are close to the Lord, you stay close to the Lord.

The serpent can try to get close through different avenues. It seems he tries something new almost every time, just to keep me guessing.

"God is more powerful." That was the best thing Father Steve ever told me. I was so worried about being taken back over by the dark one. I didn't want to go back to my old ways. I really felt worried at times that I would lose my relationship with my Savior and return to my old ways. Interesting fact: *God is more powerful than the dark one.*

"A thief comes only to steal and slaughter and destroy: I came so that they might have life and have it more abundantly." (John 10:10)

This life we live, it is a spiritual life. Most live in the world, but we are meant to look at it as a spiritual life with meaning and live *of* the world, not in it. God created us for this moment in time, not by chance, but for a reason and a purpose. Everything that happens and all the people that cross our paths are like clues in this mystery we call *life*. I am not made just to see how much work I can get done, to find my soul mate, and to fall in love and have an amazing love affair with a man. I am here on this journey to seek my Creator and to surrender and glorify God and to know and experience His amazing love.

Once I became close to Jesus and asked for forgiveness, He put me on a healing path to purify me and to become who God the Father wanted me to be, not who I thought I would be, and not to accomplish what I thought I would accomplish. Life doesn't turn out the way you thought it would because you didn't create yourself. Your personal agenda does not match God's. When you stop fighting God's plan for you that is when you will find your purpose. God created you, and He knows what he wants you to accomplish. He knows who He wants you to become. Until you surrender to Him and until you let Him drive the bus instead of you, you will not be satisfied in this life. You will always be searching for something. Everyone needs a relationship with their Creator. You will always have an empty hole in your soul, medicating it with something until you do. Whatever you think most about is what you are medicating yourself with.

My serpent was bigger maybe than others but not as big as someone else's who may have needed more rehab. For me, with a week of rehab and a couple of years of counseling, and through His healing and my surrender to Him, I was able to get the serpent off me. I wanted him off me. Until you want him off you, and until you want to seek God, you don't have a chance. Your kid or your parents or your spouse may want you to change, or they may think you are fine. You have to want it, and you have to fight for it. It is a fight to get to the light. The more you seek it, the more your darkness will fade and get smaller. I was in darkness for so long, I didn't even know I was in darkness. This is the case for most. If you are complaining, then there is some work that you need to be doing on yourself. Surrender to Jesus, and He will shine a light on your darkness. You may be in denial. Eventually He will get you to realize it.

Returning to Him is the way to stay awake spiritually. It is an everyday thing. It explains the meaning of the phrase "our daily bread" from the Our Father prayer. We need Him to feed us every day with His Word and most importantly with silence and time alone with Him. Even just a few minutes can be a great start. Some days we have much to be healed of, others not so much. If we don't spend time with Him and take the time to refuel with His love and healing, how do we go out and face the world? Everything hurts less when we are filled up with His mercy and love. We are able to extend it to the others who cross our paths.

For so long I had trouble saying no. Now I can say no just fine. The counseling helped, as did the practice of saying it. In October 2012, God gave me Cooper, my dog, to help too. Cooper actually helped me to be able to say no and not feel bad about it; it dispelled the guilt I had associated with the word *no*. Cooper was nine when we got him. God put it in my heart to get a dog. My son and I rescued him, and in a way, he rescued us. I had never had a dog. Cooper showed me unconditional love and was so sweet to cuddle with me on bad days. More importantly, he taught me to say no loudly and to mean it, over and over again. He was a strong male dog with a strong personality. Plus, he taught me boundaries, which is huge for a sex addict. I am not saying to go out and get a dog. I am saying he did teach me a lot, and I think I experienced some healing through him as well.

When I walked him in the neighborhood, I had him on a retractable leash, kind of going to the bathroom wherever he wanted on neighbors' lawns. I didn't have the leash rolled in and kept tight so he would be right by me, and I didn't know to tug on the leash and say "No!" so that he couldn't pee somewhere. I was just letting him go wherever and do whatever. I always picked up his droppings, but that wasn't quite acceptable enough with some of the neighbors. One of the neighbors let me know she didn't like it and neither did another neighbor. I thought, "If they don't like it, then others are probably mad too." Looking back, it is kind of funny to me now. No wonder they got mad. He was way up in their yard due to the retractable leash.

In that experience, I could see how I let men walk all over me and do whatever they wanted. Just as I was letting Cooper do whatever he wanted. It was me that needed fixing in all of those relationships. Whatever they need is not for me to decide or to tell them. It was the same way I was with my son. I let other people run me. I let them railroad me. It really made me realize a lot. This was a real-life application, even if it was with a dog. I soon learned that I could tell Cooper "no," and I could keep him close to me when I took him on a walk, and I could be an authoritative person. I am not a doormat any longer, and it feels amazing. It feels freeing. It doesn't happen overnight. All of this takes work. It is all a journey and a walk with God. It is getting to know Him and becoming closer to Him. Therefore, He draws you in even closer to Him. He sent me on a journey of healing, and I can share it. I know it will be different for everyone. For everyone's pain is different. If you seek Him and His help, He will guide you along a journey of healing. It will be the most amazing trip of your life!

"Your word is a lamp to my feet and a light for my path." (Psalm 119:105)

I tried hard to get someone to love me, anyone who gave me attention. First clue to my downfall: attention seeker. I sought attention by trying hard to be pretty, skinny, and fun. That one was a hard one to admit. I didn't see myself that way. But how we are and how we perceive ourselves can be two totally different things. The guys I attracted had their own wounds. I was their negative experience from childhood. I was a clingy, low self-esteem version of someone from their childhood. A caregiver probably enmeshed with them to form their issues with relationships—possibly a mom who wanted to be rescued and loved so much that she expected her child to provide what she couldn't get from her husband or lack of one. What have I done to my son?

Wounds are set by a young age. My counselor said, "Don't think about that." When you don't come clean with your kids, you have a high possibility of setting them up to repeat a version of the same painful life you had. At the very least, we can give our children the foundation and gift of faith as my parents did for me. It is my greatest treasure on Earth. My son will have that to fall back on like a soft, billowy pillow to catch him. The Blessed Mother and Jesus will be there waiting for him as they are for all of us.

My sister and her friend both said, "I know I have issues, but I don't want to know what they are." Once they knew I was in counseling, they told me that. So they realize that much; they are unhappy, but they just deal with it, as if it is just a part of life. Let God make your life, not you. Sometimes it involves getting help, and that takes courage. It definitely involves God. The reason why we need God is that we are all wounded, and it takes Jesus to heal us. Psychology is great, and it did help me to identify much of what I needed to be aware of. It pointed out patterns that I never saw and gave me red-, yellow-, and green-light behavioral signs to watch out for. Before, I was totally clueless. It was a little hard to swallow at times. They pointed out things that, I grew to realize, I had experienced over and over again in my relationships. It can seem like a different person each time, and of course they will look different. Even I would bounce between the obvious controlling guy and the more manipulative not-so-obvious-to-me controlling "nice" guy, yet I had the same experience each time.

We are all in need of counseling to a greater or lesser degree, but few choose that road. Just like we are all in need of a relationship with Jesus Christ, but few really know this or choose that road either. At least I didn't. I went to church as I was growing up, and off and on during my twenties and thirties. Maybe I was deaf to what they were saying.

I know I was blind to what was wrong in my life.

I trust in You, Lord. No longer do I fear what tomorrow may bring. No longer am I anxious; I have You, Lord, to take refuge in. I know you will take care of me, Lord. I am your beloved precious daughter. It is such a comfort to feel your love shine down on me like a ray of sunshine on a warm day. I trust you to take care of me and my son. I still need help with so much.

The nuns, priests, and lay people of my church that I have met throughout my journey have been examples to me of God's love. I was so ashamed at first to tell them my story and my past, but I know it is by the grace of God and their help and His healing and love that I was able to turn from sin. It was by God's grace that I could even recognize my sin and know enough to want to stop and get out. The evil spirit is all around us, and he is taking over people through their sins. They know something is wrong by the way they feel inside. They need our kindness. God is love, and God created all of us. He knows our sickness and our wounds, so therefore He knows why we do what we do.

"Be merciful, just as also your Father is merciful." (Luke 6:36)

My Lord, my Lord, how I love my Lord, who let me have free will to fall so deep into a dark hole on a path to hell. He pulled me out when I reached out my hand. My hand was all dirty and bruised, and He kissed it with His holy lips and said to me in a still small voice, my child, I have been waiting so long for you to come home. God whispers to me, will you help the others? Bring my lost, lonely, tender, hurting sheep home.

My reply is, "Gladly." Thy will be mine every time. I choose eternal life. I choose God. I don't have to feel bad anymore for my past. I am set free.

A prayer of thanks to God: Thank you so much for rescuing me with your love, forgiveness, and open arms. It feels so good to be home. I was lost for so long. You took away my hurt, pain, and loneliness and filled it up with your love. So much Love! So much love! I am overflowing with your love! I ask you, Lord, to please heal the wounded people reading this book. I pray for your grace to heal them and for them to draw close to you all the while you are drawing closer to them.

"Your Father who sees in secret will repay you." (Matthew 6:4)

When you hit your rock bottom in life, you are desperate, and you will do anything and try anything. It is where we find Jesus or where we finally surrender and seek Him. We then get covered with His grace to be truly sorry for what we have done. You are ready with both arms up to be pulled out of the pit. We are the lucky ones, I feel, if we can make it out of the pit. Once we are out, we are so thankful and so in love with God. For how deep our pain was, that is how deep our love is for our Savior. Ah, if we could all be so lucky to hit our rock bottom.

There are those extraordinarily lucky people who are pure and good, pretty much since birth. They didn't have to cause their own problems like I did. Maybe their families and their mental states are healthier than where I started from. The people in the middle are kind of close to God, and they believe in God. Their lives just aren't quite miserable enough to surrender to Him. They are healthy enough and have a decent savings and spouse, and so on, so that they can get by with life as it is. A few may seek a relationship with Jesus, but most will not. But those of us in misery, we will dive in. We have nothing to lose. We are at the edge of the cliff. It's time to dive into Jesus and let your old self die, so you can be made new.

I have tried to help those wounded people I spoke of. The problem is that they know everything, and they say, "Just because you are happy now, why do you think everyone else isn't?" I wish sometimes I couldn't see their pain. I can see it by their actions and the things they speak of. I see it in their eyes. But do they really hide their pain from themselves so much that they can never quite see the depth of it? It perplexes me. We all try to control something until we surrender it over to the Lord. What shade, degree or level of controller are we? Surrender to God is daily for me for this reason. How do I get others to surrender and give up the control to God? How do I say, "Your life will be so much better—trust me"? It's my own pride that thinks I can do anything at all to save them. They don't need to trust me; they need to fall in love with their Savior and trust God. Falling in love with Him is the solution to all of the problems of this world. He makes everything better. Don't take my word for it. Seek Him. Experience Him, an encounter with Him and His merciful healing graces and powerful love.

Reflecting

Twelve

HEALING

"If your right eye causes you to sin, tear it out and throw it away. It is better for you to lose one of your members than to have your whole body thrown into Gehenna."

Matthew 5:29

People have to *want* to change. They have to get to the point at which staying the same is more painful than going through the painful process of change. You spend time in school doing hard work to be successful. But then you treat yourself and your body like they are worth little. You are worth more than all the gold in the world. Picture the most beautiful place on Earth. That is how beautiful and special and important you are to him—God—your higher power. If you don't feel that way about yourself, work on yourself until you do. Then your dream of being accepted and loved will come true. Well, that was my dream. Isn't that everyone's?

Be careful of shows, music, and books that will light your fire and start the fantasy in your head. You feed your body healthy food to be healthy. What type of things are you feeding your thoughts? For some, porn can be a big problem. It wasn't for me, but there are near versions of it on television and in movies. They are triggers for me, though. What is American television doing to us and our children? Someone who is *hypersexual* like I am cannot watch that stuff. You do not just have "a high libido"—it is called hypersexual, and it is not a good thing. It is destructive for you in this life, which will lead to destruction for you in the next.

"But he was pierced for our offenses, crushed for our sins. Upon him was the chastisement that makes us whole, and by his stripes we were healed." (Isaiah 53:5)

A couple months after I got back from rehab, I went to a retreat with my Catholic2Catholic church group. There was a priest there, Father Sean, from Companions of the Cross. He spoke to us about becoming intentional disciples, which means that if you see people who are in need of some help, you help them in whatever way the Holy Spirit directs you. It could be as simple as smiling at someone who looks angry or emotionally hurt—someone you wouldn't normally go out of your way to acknowledge. At the end of the retreat, Father Sean told us he would be praying over anyone who would like to be prayed for. I had gotten into a conversation with someone and nearly missed the opportunity. I started in the direction where he was going to be praying over people, and I crossed his path. We went back and sat down. I told him about my struggles with sex addiction and my rehab experience.

He said, "Psychology is great, but Jesus heals." He put his hand on my forehead and prayed for me and then stopped to ask if I felt anything. I told him I felt purification; it was like this washing feeling from my head down to my toes, ever so slowly and slightly. He continued to pray over me more as tears fell from my eyes. It was amazing to experience the cleansing of my soul. My struggles with my addiction were lightened by that experience. He continued to pray over me every time I saw him. I am so thankful that Jesus healed me through him. And just by doing that to me, Father Sean taught me how to pray over people and bring God's peace to those with the faith to receive it.

I was at a water park with my son, where a little girl's leg got cut, and she was bleeding and in need of stitches. Her mom was trying to get her calm enough to leave the water park. I asked her mom if they believed in God, and if so, whether I could pray over the little girl. The mom agreed, and I placed my hands on that little girl's leg and prayed, and she stopped screaming and crying. One of the other moms said, "Can you do that to all of our kids?" I have done that to adults, but it seems to work better the younger the person is. Maybe it is because they are fresh from God without the doubts that the world brings. It makes me think of the scripture in Mark 10:52, when Jesus told Bartimaeus, "Go your way; your faith has saved you." Before I pray, I ask for the Holy Spirit to come and give thanks to Jesus and ask for the prayer to be answered in Jesus name. Prayer is powerful!

In a small voice God tells me to Him you are worth more than gold. He loves ALL his children this much. Share your story of desperation, healing, and hope with them. Tell them if they would only come to Me and surrender their lives to Me, how much I can help them and love them. And let them know, even if they don't now, that I still love them always, even on their worst sinful days. I should wish they would turn to Me and tell me, 'Sorry, Father. Please, Father, please help me.' Because you know, Dawn, I can help them. Just as I have freed you and broken your chains of addiction and bondage to sin and despair. I can help all of them.

So this is my mission. I am the messenger of His love. I am the proof that no matter how big the sin, just as the stories in the gospels of Matthew, Mark, Luke, and John, he forgives. Jesus is alive and here today, just as he was over two thousand years ago. We are running out of time. The evil one has clutched onto so many, as he was onto me.

"Beware that your hearts do not become drowsy from carousing and drunkenness and the anxieties of daily life, and that day catch you by surprise." (Luke 21:34)

I was in so much darkness. In one of my meditations, a demon or the devil flew off me. But I had to wiggle and fight to get him off me. He was like an octopus. He didn't want to let go. I had to want him off me. I had to want to stop the sin. I had to want to turn to my Heavenly Father. Nobody could make me do this. I did it on my own. Just as every one of you has to. I hated who I was, and I wanted out. I couldn't end my life because I had a son. I chose to live, but I did have to die to my worldly self. I wanted to be like Scarlett O'Hara and have power and control over men. To me, they were an object to be consumed and discarded. I didn't really think I felt that way. It was covered up with "Oh, I want to fall in love!" The way I was living, it was nothing about love. It was about looking at people as objects and objectifying myself. It was about lust and power and control. It was all consuming. It was all I cared about: to be in love. It was what the evil one had me believe, and it was all lies. He lied to me, and he is lying to you. Maybe sex, relationships, and masturbation aren't your problem. But what is?

If you are not with God, then the evil spirit has some power over you. There is something he is lying to you about. There is something missing from your life, causing some very empty feeling, and you are filling it up with something. You are putting something before God. Something that you don't want to let go of, that you think you can't live without.

What we don't like in another is what we hide from ourselves. For so long, I felt hatred and disgust toward controlling people, not seeing at all how controlling I was. I saw myself as an easygoing person who would do whatever whenever with nearly whoever to get what I wanted, which was their love. But that wasn't real. I felt resentment toward the person I was giving myself to after a time. Then the resentment turned into hatred. It was horrible. Nothing lasted. I was the common denominator in all the chaos. Every guy I dated, I ended up hating—never once thinking it had anything to do with me. It is wise to say it takes two, and there are three sides to every story. I wasn't healthy, so I attracted men who were not healthy either. Most of us need healing of some sort. We attract the same experience over and over again. My ex-fiancé and ex-husband appeared to be different in many, many ways. Not just physically, but even in the way they treated me. The same experience for me was in a repeated pattern, not just with them but in general with the men I dated. They ignored me after a time. They were controlling and didn't respect my opinion or value my feelings as a person. It was the same experience I had as a child. We try to heal our childhood wounds through our partners. Yet some people get lucky—50 percent, I suppose, as it appears statistically from those who stay married. Of those, how many are happy? They are happy enough or deal with it and make it work. If they both had God and realized on both sides they were attracted to each other primarily due to the negative traits from childhood, could they heal and their marriage become all that God wants their marriage to be?

With God in your relationships, I believe this to be true, and it can happen. So maybe those are the 3 percent that people joke about who actually are happily married. What about everyone else? They are not into working on themselves or their marriage, and so they kind of just go through life dealing with it. But I see the pain and misery it builds. By the time people are in their fifties, it is overwhelming for some. This is often when addictions start to rear their ugly heads. It starts at all different ages, but by now the monster is big. They have gotten used to their way of living. That is life? It doesn't have to be. There is a cure, and

His name is Jesus Christ. People try so many things to make their lives better. We work out, party, buy things, or work a lot. We try so much and so many different things. We spend so much money trying different ways to help. Why, oh, why won't they try Him out? What are they so afraid of and against? They say they believe in God or they have always been close to God. I was one of these people; I get it. You just don't know that there is a way to go deeper.

You don't know you have to go deeper for it to work, for it to really work. You have to give up control. Frankly, we have so many control freaks. It is because we are wounded. The longer we let these wounds go and fester, the harder it is to heal them. But it is not impossible. Through Christ, all things are possible. People work on their education and go to school and get smart. They want to build up their bank accounts, get a great job, collect money, save, and invest. This is the American way. Educational costs have skyrocketed, and we tell our children they have to go to college. You have to succeed. We seek perfection, and this is where the big problem is created. We can only become perfect through Christ. Any other type of perfection-seeking is destructive and dangerous. When we mess up—and we will, we plummet as if we are diving off a burning building. When we hit the ground,

we hit hard. We are not used to this. We beat ourselves up with all those voices we heard as kids.
They come back to us. They are deadly. How we
feel matches up to the voices in our heads, and we
believe it. It is the evil one's way, part of his perfect
plan to get us into his clutches. In order to begin
feeling better, we go to our comforts of choice. Basically and unknowingly, we go to our dark sides.

There is only one Savior, and He is waiting for you: Jesus. He is my lover now. Not in the
traditional way one would think of a lover. I love
Him, and He heals me perpetually in this life on
Earth. Our way is hell on Earth. His way is heaven
on Earth. Do you know this? Once you know this,
what will you choose? For when we don't know and
all we know is control and trying to do the best we
can, it takes us on a highway to hell. There are no
exits. Usually the only way is to crash and hit rock
bottom. Addicts have a good chance of this. But a
rainbow can appear if they seek the one who created them. Then they will fall into the arms of the
Savior, who can heal and restore and redeem and
make them new. Then in the desperation of the
crash, when they have nowhere else to go, they have
a better chance than most at seeking Him. But will
they stay? Are they aware that in the next step to
all this, they have the enemy watching them like a

hawk? Waiting for the right moment to suck them back in? He will try to get you back into his hold. The good news is that God is more powerful, but you have to turn it up. You have to seek Him more and pray more and find ways of seeking His perfect protection. You have to *choose* to fight for this and seek help when you feel the spiritual attack.

"Peace I leave with you; my peace I give unto you. Not as the world gives, do I give it to you. Do not let your heart be troubled or afraid." (John 14:27)

You know when I got deeper into this and learned about spiritual warfare and had people tell me about attacks by the evil spirit, I thought, "What freaks! What are they talking about?" I had no idea! I only ever believed in God. I never thought about the evil guy. I don't even want to say his name. But if you believe in God, you have to believe in the opposite of him. If you are not with God and close to God, then have you ever thought about just who you are with and close to? You have to be *aware*. Who are you feeding? We seem to go through life on automatic pilot. The evil guy then gets easy access to us. He takes us over. We have to seek God to overpower him. God is always there with His army of angels to fight him, but we have to ask. We have to want it. God wants us to talk to Him. What do you want? Do you know? Are you aware? We must have a relationship with ourselves to discover just whom we are close to. For if you discover you don't have a relationship with Jesus, then just who from the spirit world are you having relations with?

I remember when I went to counseling and told my therapist I was seeking counseling due to the fact that I was sick and tired of all of my broken relationships that never lasted. I wanted a long-term relationship, for the rest of my life. She stared at me in a loving way; this is how you know you have a good counselor. You need to connect and feel their love and compassion. Your soul can sense being judged just as it can sense compassion. It knows the difference deep within you.

She said, "How about you work on a relationship with yourself?"

I thought, "Wow, I never thought of that before. What the heck does she mean by that?"

It was profound to me. What a concept. But I don't like to be alone. I don't know how I really feel about anything. I never realized I didn't like to feel! I thought I was a touchy-feely person. That was all evil guy hype too.

I was always the girl next door. This is typical with those who have lust as their main idol. Our values and morals don't match with our behavior. We can look all prim and proper and even act it. You would never know. Typically with the lust factor, you may talk about it a lot in certain circles because it is there on your brain. But you can hide it from the people you have to when you want to. It is easy. Masturbation and living in your head and fantasies are such easy things to keep from others. They are so private. Nobody talks about it. To most, it is their idea of normal. It is a way of functioning. It offers relief and gives temporary balance when life seems to be unbearable due to the stress of a partner, work, family, or friends. Who will know? Sometimes the partner ventures out to others and is caught—then it becomes a more obvious problem to the outside world, like eating or drinking too much, or doing drugs, or overspending due to shopping or gambling. But what if you can manage all that, and you work a lot so you don't have much time for any of that, even if that was second nature? Masturbation and fantasy become an easy escape. It is similar to those who have several drinks when they get home to unwind. It is accepted due to the fact that the evil one lies to us. He wants you to die from your misery, in some form or another. He doesn't want you to have peace and joy. If you were at peace, you wouldn't seek his pleasure fillers. You would have joy and wouldn't need it. Peace is something people do not realize they can get through Jesus Christ.

Thirteen

PARENTING

"You judge by appearances, but I do not judge anyone."

John 8:15

I wanted a dad who would adore me and call me his darling and tell me he loved me. I wanted a dad who liked spending his time hanging out with me, doing what I liked at times, even if he didn't like what I wanted to do. I wanted a dad who would want to hug me tight as a boa constrictor, and never let me go, as if his life depended on hugging me. I wanted that kind of hug. I wanted him to call me and say, "How was your day?" I wanted him to end the conversation with, "I love you, sweetheart." That was what I wanted. That is not what I got. I told him that was what I wanted. Well, most of it, the phone calls and "I love you" part. I saw anger in his eyes when I told him this. He shows love in the way that he feels he is loved. He fixes things around my house. He helped me move at least nine times since high school. He helped me move home every summer from college and every fall back to college. He would fix my car and do all the little "honey do" tasks on my list at my home since I didn't have a man to do them. What does he want from me? To feel loved, the same way back that he gives it. He likes it when

I help him around his house. I had to accept and forgive him that he did not know how I needed to be loved. Now I accept him and love him for who he is and for who he isn't. The more unconditional love I show him, the better our relationship is.

Gary D. Chapman wrote a book called *The Five Love Languages*, a guide for couples, about what people's love languages are. I think mine is touch and words of positive affirmation. When a kid's love language is touch and they get spanked and that is pretty much the only touch they get, it is very harmful to them. Or if a kid's love language is words of positive affirmation, but mostly all they get is criticism, it is very harmful to the child. So I get it now. I get why I felt hatred toward my dad. I get it why I felt so much anger toward him. When I was in rehab, a lot of that came out. I didn't even know it was in me. I had to come to terms with the fact that I was mad at my mom too, for not stopping him, even though that was the hardest for me to see of the two. I feel I am repeating the pattern since I am not married anymore to my son's father. When my son's father is in a bad mood and takes it out on my son, he doesn't have me there to protect him. We repeat our parents. I am not blaming my parents at all. They did the best they could do in spite of the wounds they carry around from their own wounded childhoods. We all do. Do we heal them? Do we figure out why we aren't happy and why we do what we do? Or do we medicate and ignore and just think this is life? Life doesn't have to be this hard. No matter the storm, you can have peace in the trial.

I don't want my parents' good points to go unmentioned. It's easy in life to focus on only the negative traits in those closest to us, just as it is easier to see the good traits in someone we barely know. My father is the hardest-working person I have known or will ever know. He is nearly eighty now, so he is slowing down, but he used to barely sit and enjoy himself. He opened his own business, a gas station, when he was twenty-five, and then he bought the gas station across the street, which had a repair shop with it. My mom told me he used to work outside in the cold on big trucks. That is why he bought the gas station across the street, because he wanted to work on cars on the inside of a building in the winter. He had a tow truck for a while and would have to get up in the middle of the night and go help people who were stranded. In the '60s he had a nervous breakdown, and the doctor told him he needed to learn to rest and do something other than work. After that, my parents bought the lake house up north, which was more work for them, but at least it added some restful times.

Many people tell my mom she is a saint. She is seventy-five years old now. She used to be very easygoing, but in the last five years or so, she has come out of her shell and has a backbone now. I am not sure if that came with age or talking to her about my transformation. I don't remember her asking for anything or wanting anything; she was content with nothing due to how poor her family was. When she was growing up, she used to have to wash out her socks and underwear at night and cover up with coats in the winter, so she said she was happy to have a warm home. Her favorite thing to do, she said, was to go to the grocery store and buy whatever she wanted. When she and my dad were first married, they had to figure out exactly how much their groceries were going to be before they went up to the checkout since they only had a little bit of money. She said she was like the girl in the *Coal Miner's Daughter* movie and just about wore her clothes under her pajamas on her wedding night. She was scared to have sex. It's hard for her to know my story. She doesn't understand it. She wants to know what she did wrong.

I said, "Mom, you and dad have your wounds from childhood, and you did the best you guys could do raising me with those hurts you had no idea you had. Add that to the culture of our society the way it is. It just makes for the perfect storm." It's nobody's fault because nobody did anything on purpose. Just like my son will need Jesus and possibly professional help one day. I did the best that I could do, but I am humble enough to know I have done a lot wrong and will do a lot wrong in the future. I wasn't healthy when he was little. I didn't go to rehab until he was eight, plus parenting is not easy.

I can't take back the damage I did to him and the wounds I created for him. I didn't do it on purpose, for I didn't know I was sick. I am not sick anymore, and I will take responsibility for however his life turns out, and I will have to be at peace with it. The hard part for my son will be figuring out what healing he is in need of. Only God can show us that, in His light. That is the bridge to Jesus and to being saved. Our brokenness and suffering, for most, are the only reasons we will seek our Savior. My son is smart and has a very strong personality, like his father. He has to be given a good reason for anything I ask him to do. It is that very same type of personality that has a hard time opening up, trusting, and surrendering to our Lord. It is the very type of personality that needs our Creator's love so much, just as each and every one of us do.

You do have to do the work to get to know your Shepherd. You do have to put in the time.

He will have you give up the worldly things that you *think* you love. I thought I loved orgasms and feeling my naked body up against another naked body. But I came to find out that was the devil's lie. I would feel bad about myself after, with the guilt and the shame. Maybe not immediately after, because it would sometimes creep up on me over time, even if I felt as if I were in love, so I could justify it. But then t would catch up to me and hit me like a brick. At the end of the relationship, there would be a movie of all the things we did—all the things I did to please him, and all the things I thought he would like so that he would love me for them and never leave me. That movie would play over and over again in my head. It is disgusting.

My Heavenly Father tells me in that still small voice, my darling, you have to let them go. In order to heal and to love yourself, you must leave the past behind you. My Son was tortured and crucified so you do not have to hang onto any of that. The evil one would love for me to stay at the bottom of my pit of hell. That is not pleasing to my Heavenly Father. He gave me His son's hand and grabbed me and wrapped me into his warm embrace, and He won't let go of me unless I let go of Him first. His love compares to no one and nothing. His compassion and mercy are beyond anything you can imagine. He is waiting for you. You! No matter what past you have—he doesn't care. He wants you to give up your sins and what you think you love. What you think you love may be killing you. You may really find you don't love it, that you actually loathe it. Then you will see the others in pain all around you. You will know what can help them, but few will listen. It will be painful to watch, and you will pray and pray for them. We all have our own journey. You will have to be careful what you say to them, as it will seem like you are judging them.

The evil one will twist what you say and what they hear, so that you seem to be self-righteous to them, when all you want for them is what our Heavenly Father wants for all of us. You want them to experience heaven on Earth. You want them to stop living in the hell they are in. You want them to turn to our Father and say, "I am home, and I am so sorry. Please forgive me and help me to forgive myself."

This "thorn in my flesh," that Paul speaks of in 2 Corinthians 12:7, keeps me close to our Lord, and it keeps me humble. Therefore, I look to it as my blessing. I didn't used to see it this way. It doesn't become your gift until you realize you need a Savior, and you give your life to Him. It is my gift and blessing, for it was the only way I would surrender my life over to our Lord, and it remains my gift and blessing for it keeps me hanging on to Jesus's hand. I now understand why I need him and why my thorns and suffering are my greatest blessings. They led me to the light of my eternal life that I can now look forward to and not be afraid of. Do you know your thorns? The evil one knows them, and he uses them against us. We feel it is who we are, but it's not. That is his deception. Jesus knows who we really are, even if we don't yet.

PARENTING

Fourteen

SUFFERING

"Let the one among you who is without sin be the first to throw a stone at her."

John 8:7

God has us go through suffering to draw us closer to Him. Some people are close to Him without that. But for the majority, it is some loss that draws us in, something we need to trust Him on, something we need to have faith in Him about, so we know that we won't die from our pain and that He is there. He will get us through. This increases our faith, and we cling to him because we feel if we don't, we will die. We will kill ourselves in some way, shape, or form to end the pain, even if it's a slow death through a destructive way of living. But with Him, we somehow know instinctively that He will ease our suffering. He will give us the grace to get through it. When we share our stories, someone else doesn't feel all alone. It is what community really means, to share in each other's suffering and to know that there is more to life than suffering. It is to know that in helping others we heal ourselves. That is why there is more joy in giving than in receiving. To be a giver and ease the pain of another is what life is about. Or that is what life *should* be about. We do not have enough givers in this world.

It feels as if the evil one is taking over. Maybe it has always felt that way. It feels that way to me because the takers are overriding the givers. People feel entitled to things. People feel it is owed to them, or they deserve it. They have a "why can't I have it now" mentality. So what will happen to our world when there are only takers left? Nobody will know how to give because nobody will see anyone else giving to learn from it. We will all be too busy with our own lives to give of ourselves for another. Doesn't it seem to be headed that way already? We have to get our stuff done, and we have to work a lot of hours at work, and we have to save money and keep getting more money, for we worry about the future.

We take, and we don't give because we don't trust. We live in a state of fear. Fear of the unknown. When we live without the Lord—this is how we live. I know, for I lived this way too. I was scared to write the book. What will people think of me? The people who judge me, well, I know what is going on there. It will still hurt the human side of me, though. Once you are living in the spiritual world, you understand much as to why things are the way they are and why people do and say and live the way they do. When it is about you, and it affects you and your family, it hurts. You can't get away from the human ego. You can pull it off and constantly be aware, but it is always trying to reattach, kind of like the evil guy. Maybe they go hand in hand.

Before my surrender, it was ridiculous how much I pushed myself and how much I tried to get done. I would put so much on my list. My roommate after college would say, "You can't possibly get all of that done." I was setting myself up for failure. That is how I would feel. I could work twelve hours a day on a Saturday doing things around the house, but as you know, you are never done. I would actually feel bad about what I didn't get done. I could be diligent at my employment all day long and go home dwelling on the thing I didn't get done. I would go back in ready to do it all over again, feeling the same. It was like I was on that wheel the gerbil gets on, and it spins and spins and spins. He doesn't go anywhere. It doesn't look like fun. It looks like all he does is tire himself out. You work really hard to try to get the accolades and awards and money, as if to say to everyone, "Look at me! Look at all this stuff I have. Look at how nice my clothes are and how pretty my face is." I wonder about the people who look the best out there and dress the best and work so hard to look good and have the best—do they feel the worst inside? They are hard to please. Try living in that head. They are impossible to please to themselves. I know this; this is me—or it *was* me.

When you like yourself, you will know you are the loved, beloved child of God. You don't need the boob job or the fancy car, the clothes, the house, etc. You don't need any of that. You feel good because you are loved and because you know who loves you. Suddenly it didn't matter if I bought my clothes at Meijer's or Nordstrom's, or if I drove an old car or a brand-new car. Suddenly I didn't want anything! Wait, let me say that one more time. *Suddenly I didn't want anything.* Do you know how good that feels to not long for someone else's life? To not long for someone else's car or house or spouse or kid or job or body? Once you know He loves you, and I mean He really loves you, and you believe Him and trust Him, then you become satisfied. You don't want anything. It is an amazing feeling. But then you know what He does because He is a generous God? Once you don't want anything, and you are happy with your life and so happy that He loves you, and you have gratitude for all He has given you, even your suffering because it made you a way better person— He blesses you! I mean, He always has. But this time you are seeing the blessings. And you are noticing them, and you are thanking Him, and He is blessing you with more and more. He blesses you with little things or sometimes big, really cool and amazing blessings. Your life just suddenly works, and you see the results because your life is getting easier.

He is guiding you along on a path. With God, you have so much without wanting anything. You realize what you do have is His love that pours out of you. You want to help others because of this realization. You become a giver. Not just of money and things. I am talking about you. You give yourself, your love. When you have the love of God in you, His love overflows out of you like an endless and timeless waterfall. You are a spouting fountain of it. You see people hurting, and you begin to pray for them even if you don't know them. Sometimes I find the courage to ask if I can pray over them. When people are hurting, they are so open to this comfort. When it is from the Holy Spirit, God knows who will receive Him, and that is who He tells me to approach and ask if I can pray over them. Prayer is powerful, and it is known because people have seen the miracles and the results of it.

As people, we do the things we do because we are wounded. When we judge others, we are showing we lack compassion for ourselves. We would have to have compassion for our own faults before we could have compassion for someone else's shortcomings. I used to be such a critical person. Especially of the men I dated. Once the pedestal fell and broke, the criticizing would come. It was never to their faces. No. That would have given them the ability to defend themselves. The abandonment I was afraid of. I would do it to them first. I would walk away, never having to really commit myself, keeping the fear of getting hurt at bay, which ended up hurting even more over time. We all have that hurt of some sort. We hurt inside, and we continue to hurt ourselves by how we treat ourselves and the way in which we live our lives and treat our bodies. Then we continue to hurt others. We don't see it that way. We don't even see that we are hurting ourselves. Even when we do, at that point we are too far gone. It appears too hard to stop, too hard to quit whatever it is we are poisoning ourselves with. That is the evil guy's lies again. Jesus is almighty and powerful, and He wants to save us all and wants us all to join Him in heaven. He wants to see us joyful on Earth and to show others that heaven is on Earth.

I feel sadness for our society now. Many women think they have to be sex symbols to get men. They think they have to like or love sex to get men to like or love them. They will even brainwash themselves that they love sex, and it is so important to them. They have confused sex and love. They want love. To get love, they have sex. They aren't really getting love. It is fake, superficial intimacy. It starts a pattern, a habit that may turn into an addiction.

Girls like me, we are addicted to hope. Not the kind God offers. I am thankful to be introduced to that kind. The kind of hope addiction I am talking of is unhealthy. We put so much hope in the wrong things and wrong people. We believe it will be different. We buy all their excuses, and we forgive. We have really big hearts, for we are addicted to love. The kind of love we are addicted to is an empty, superficial kind of love. Women aren't made to be this way, for God created us to be the carriers of life. We are love.

The evil guy is destroying the family life in the world through sex. It is all accepted by our culture. If you want our culture to change, start loving people. Meet people where they are. It is hard, but we have to remember it is a journey. God is so patient with us. We can learn so much from him. All of us can. You may not get the timing he has for someone. I was ready at twenty-eight to get pulled into him, or so I thought. I just wasn't ready to do the work yet. I was desperate, on my knees, pleading with him, "God, I am so lonely, and I am so empty. Please help me. Please, Lord, I don't want to be a ho. I don't want to be this person. I don't want to have sex with my dates too soon." I wanted to love the Lord, not sex. It was another ten years until I hit my ultimate rock bottom and got serious about getting out of the pit.

For those who don't realize they live in darkness, for those who don't realize their lives could be better and that he makes everything better—how do you explain it to them? How do you get your point across so they want to try him out? They like to try new restaurants and casinos and stores. But to try having a deeper relationship with the Lord, the one guy who for sure can save them—they aren't so interested in that. It's like I have this information. I have real living proof. I was in pain. I sought comfort through the arms of men who were also in pain. We pretended it was about companionship, about falling in love and finding a mate. It all started with having sex, not just before marriage but way too soon into the relationship, if you can even call it a relationship. If everyone lived aware and knew they were in pain, then would they seek Him? I think most don't even realize they are in pain. When you've lived that way for so long, how would you know?

I am joyful. I am a better mom. I no longer long for material things. Now I realize the blessings instead of thinking of what I don't have. It is not forced. I just see it. It's like I went through life with blinders on, and now they are gone. I went through life only being able to hear and see certain things. When guys said not-so-nice things to me in the beginning of dating, I only heard what I wanted to hear. I ignored them hitting on other girls or checking out other women in front of me. One guy called me at ten o'clock to come up to the bar with him and his friends. I asked him why he had changed his mind to invite me, and he said, "Well there are no other good-looking girls here." I wasn't even in a relationship with him yet. I just smiled and ignored it. Sounds stupid, I know, but I wanted him to love me. I wanted a relationship with him. It makes me sick. I think that is why at the end of a relationship my anger and resentment was so large. It was a buildup from the very beginning. It was stored in my internal computer in my brain. I ignored the data until the illusion was no longer there. The façade eroded. I was left with reality, and I didn't like it. Because I didn't like it, I added to it, to justify why I didn't even want to try to work on the relationship. But really, was there ever a relationship there to begin with?

Maybe you have to hit your rock bottom. Everyone's rock bottom is different. What if you didn't have to wait for that? The key is you have to actually be sorry for your sins and be able to *recognize* them; that takes God's grace. You have to want your serpent to die and to love the Lord more than your sin. First you have to recognize your sin, stop justifying it, and stop living in denial. You don't even mean to live in denial. You could say the evil one is the *king* of denial. He is the father of lies, and that is as close to denial as you will get.

I finally get now what it means to be saved, and why it is such a big deal that Jesus died for us on a cross, a person without sin who was tortured and crucified. Romans 5:8 says, "But God proves his love for us in that while we were still sinners Christ died for us." Why did God the Father sacrifice his only Son? He did it for all of us. He did it out of love, His love. We as humans cannot live without it to feel whole. We are all unworthy, but His grace grants us this. I was someone with huge sins and many of them. I am still a sinner. God is revealing them to me to continue my conversion to become like Him. The part about me being this huge sinner—I didn't really realize it. That is where the father of lies comes from. He keeps us in denial about what we are doing to ourselves. It is like a slow, painful death. Really he is torturing us, but he sugarcoats it with pleasure. We think we have great lives. We accept the pain that is with it as part of life. We don't realize we are inflicting our own pain by the way we live, a way of life without a relationship with Jesus Christ. The devil wants us for all eternity, as slaves. He doesn't care that he is hurting us. He loves to see us in pain, and he loves to watch us inflict ourselves with our own pain. He is the catalyst of our destructive ways. He is twisted, so he is able to twist the appearance. Shopping will make us happy, and so will drinking, gambling, sex, drugs, or whatever it is. We think, "Oh, this will be a good time." How we know it is from the evil spirit is that it starts to consume us and takes us over. It leads us to nothing good, be it a hangover, credit card debt, our health, loss of those we love, or death. Everything that comes from God leads to something good. When it is of the evil spirit, it leads to something bad. A hangover is bad. A huge credit card bill you can't pay with items on it you didn't need is bad. How I would feel after I had sex with someone is bad. I never realized it was from the devil. When you help someone, you feel good. That is from God.

The dark one has us all blind, so blind. Most people, after time, figure out that they cause their own problems. My father pointed that out to me decades ago, and it is so true. It is because we are feeding the wrong spirit. We don't even realize we are inviting the evil spirit in to take up residency in our souls. The reality is that this is what most of us do without knowing it. You have to realize you are in hell on Earth. Instead trade it in for more of heaven on Earth! Jesus is very much alive and within us like He was when He walked around on Earth over two thousand years ago. We can have a relationship with Him today. It comes from realizing the evil guy has taken us over. It comes from not wanting to live the way we live, and wanting to do something about it! It is telling Jesus we are sorry and asking Him to forgive us. It is asking Him to grant us the grace to change our ways. It is asking for His help to be obedient and to be able to live the way He wants us to live. You have to believe, and you have to trust Him. You have to want the life He wants for you—thy will be mine, Lord. If you ask Jesus to reveal to you what your darkness is, He will. In wanting to seek Him, it happens. He shows you. For it is the only way to form a relationship with Him.

SUFFERING

Fifteen

NARCISSISM

"For God, who said, 'Let light shine out of darkness,' has shone in our hearts to bring to light the knowledge of the glory of God on the face of Jesus Christ."

2 Corinthians 4:6

I used to be very critical of everyone, forever seeing everyone else's issues, yet I was blind to my own. It was a way for me to escape, to look at someone else and see what was wrong with everybody else. I read the book *Malignant Self-Love: Narcissism Revisited*, by Sam Vaknin. I read that book three times, and it is over five hundred pages long. I never saw myself in those pages. In rehab they told me I had narcissistic traits. I was an inverted narcissist, a codependent. It explains why I attracted the people I attracted. I about fell over. Of everything that I was blind to, that one topped them all.

I held a lot of shame, thinking that I was a bad person, thinking that I had to put on a front so that people would like me. I didn't think that if I was myself anybody would like me. Not being true to me became my everyday personality; I didn't realize I was doing this, and it was exhausting. Because of it, I liked my time alone. I never thought of myself as a fake person. I always said I didn't like fake people. That is exactly who I was—fake, not real, telling you what you wanted to hear so that you would like me. I didn't feel worthy of love or worthy of much of anything, not even a guy taking me out to dinner. I didn't want a guy to take me to dinner because I didn't want to "owe him." Narcissism is very hard to see in oneself. It sums up all of the negative traits nobody wants to admit they have: self-absorption, attention seeking, and usually an addiction of some sort, to name just a few.

Narcissists seek perfection. When someone points out that they are not perfect in some way, shape or form, it causes much pain for them. It is why most never seek therapy. Drive down the street and check out the yards or houses where it is like a museum—a narcissist may live there. There are different shades of it. Mostly we are people who want to look perfect and have the best and want it all and seek perfection in everything we do. We run companies and make for great employees on the surface. We have a drive to be number one. We lack empathy, and we objectify ourselves and everyone we encounter. We are addicted to power and control, whether obvious or not so obvious. There is a cerebral and somatic kind (sexual) of narcissism. The somatic narcissist is obsessed with his or her body and looking good. You will find me at the gym. The cerebral narcissist is into being the smartest person, the know-it-all.

It took me six years from the time I read *Malignant Self-Love* until I went to therapy to discover I had many traits of a narcissist, and only when a professional pointed it out to me. My therapist said, "You can learn empathy," since narcissists lack it. I didn't think of myself as someone who was not empathetic. Looking back, all I did was judge, complain, and criticize everyone and everything. It seemed I could either lead a group or follow, but I was never able to just join in and be a part of one, which explains my attention seeking. I required lots of attention and wanted to be the best-looking girl in the room. We are competitive. I have been told there is no cure for narcissistic personality disorder. There are varying shades and degrees of narcissism, and a small percentage of people have the actual disorder. I was told a narcissist would be the last person who would stay in treatment or ever seek treatment. You can't help people get better who don't think they need any help. Jesus can help us with our lives. It's hard for the narcissists of the world to get close to God, for they think they don't need Him. If we can get our culture to seek God, then we could heal the narcissism in the world. Jesus takes us out of our self-absorption. So maybe it is true that a psychiatrist or psychologist cannot cure narcissism, but Jesus can cure anything He wants to.

Those who talk about others and judge and are critical display traits of narcissism. I hope one day they have the courage to face their pain. For that is when they can work through it. It may take hitting rock bottom; sometimes I feel those of us who do are the lucky ones. At least the mask is off, and we have nowhere to turn but to God. It is as if we leave the door open to Him finally. We have no choice, yet it is our greatest gift. It is our ultimate blessing, to be so hurt that the only way to mend is to let our Creator pick up the pieces and slowly heal us and put us back together again. He puts us back together and restores us and makes us new with his love. Along the way, we learn his mercy, compassion, and forgiveness. He is so kind to us—He teaches us how to finally be that way to ourselves. In turn, we can be this way to everyone else. I used to think that seeing other people's pain was a burden, and that there was so much darkness in the world. Now I realize that to see pain is a gift. It is to see the loving and merciful heart of the Lord in action if only you would let Him. He loves us enough to let us suffer and hurt so that we can experience that much love from Him. For how great our pain is, that is how much love we get to experience with Him. For most of us, it is the only way we will ever seek Him out. I would never want to live my life over again without the pain. For then I would have to live it over again without the deep love that Jesus has for me and I have for Him. For Him to love me this much and for me to love Him to that depth grants me the grace to love everyone this much. That is a gift, for when you love that much, you receive that much love back. This is what our Creator made us for—to love one another, to be so full of His love that it spills over like a grand, overflowing waterfall. To have your pain, anger, resentment, jealousy, and envy released, to feel as free as a bird that flies in the sky—this is what you are missing out on by living in the world. There isn't money that can buy this love. There is nothing that can measure in comparison to this kind of freedom. As we go on through life and get hurt or hurt another, once we have a relationship with the Shepherd, we don't have to hang onto the pain and hurt. We then know who can help us and who can heal us. I no longer have fear, for I know who loves me and takes care of me, and I know where I am going and where my ultimate home is. It is the most amazing experience. Before I got to that point, I was broken. I am grateful. I wish for everyone to hit rock bottom so they crawl into the arms of their Creator.

Will some people along the way identify with this story and see themselves in me? I can only hope this will happen. It is why I write this, to be a light in a dark world, to shine a light on someone's life story so that person seeks the Lord with all their heart, mind, body, and soul and doesn't have to live in dark pain any longer. There is a Savior, and His name is Jesus Christ. He is our Healer, and He redeems us. We don't have to carry around that old baggage, even when we feel as if we have nowhere to turn. That is when the light begins to seep in through the cracks of the dark, lonely, empty room of our soul.

The worst of things that have happened to me over my life have been such blessings. They were clues to a puzzle that I wouldn't have figured out without them. Everything that happens to us is another key to a door that will tell us something to give us a clue to our puzzle. To complete your puzzle is to see your light and your dark side. That is when your spiritual journey really begins, when you know the part of you that you need to parent and be kind to. It is the part of you that you need to feed items of the light to, like truth, love, and compassion. You also know the part of you that is a mask, is the ego, the false self. To be able to pull the mask off or let it fall so that it breaks, this is when your healing begins and you can become all that God created you to be. This is your day to turn from ashes to gold! To know your darkness keeps it small. For when you know it, then you know what

NOT to feed it. Before, you didn't know. You fed it by accident. It is exactly what the dark one wants, for you to stay in the dark; he doesn't want you to know the truth about yourself or your family or to have light shine on your darkness. He wants you to feed the monster. The bigger the monster, the harder and longer it takes to kill the serpent. Look at your parents; really see them. Ask them questions. Some won't want to tell you how they lived their lives. Maybe they still hide it, even from themselves.

"But I say to you, love your enemies, and pray for those who persecute you, that you may be children of your heavenly Father." (Matthew 5:44)

I don't have to be weak and give my power away. As Pope Francis stated, "We cannot trust in our strength, but only in Jesus and his mercy." I exhausted myself, smiling and being overly friendly to everyone, filling the role of the jester. I don't want to now, so I don't. Before I felt I had to, and I was compelled to. The less pain I had on the inside, the less I smiled on the outside. It may have been less, but it was genuine. Through those smiles God's love penetrated out into the dark world. My hope is for every person out there, whether man or woman, boy or girl, to know their self-worth.

To know your self-worth is to know whom you belong to, and you belong to God. You are a child of God. I used to say, "If only we could bottle up self-worth and pass it out for people to take." It was in me all along, as it is in you. It just takes accepting Jesus's love and mercy. It is a vaccine for all of the sickness inside of you, inside of our world.

The hardest and biggest lesson I have learned is that you have to be blunt and direct with men. Or at least that was true of the men that I attracted. I sent mixed signals because I didn't want to hurt their feelings. Or maybe the mixed signals were from the tug-of-war struggle going on inside of me between my darkness and what was left of my light side. Now I know you have to be honest, direct, and tell it like it is. Jesus taught me that the truth will set you free, and that it does. I have had some scary situations with men. One time I even unknowingly got involved with a stalker. I went on a few dates with him and realized he had major anger issues. He had a hard time with leaving me alone. He would call my cell phone every minute for an hour. He threatened to strangle me with a scarf. He said he was going to crush my head like it was an orange. I went to the police and showed the officer my phone. He called the guy and told him to leave me alone. He told the officer that I was calling him.

The officer said, "I looked at all of the incoming and outgoing calls on her phone. I know what is going on. Leave her alone." I was so close to getting a personal protection order against him. The officer said a phone call from them usually worked, and it did.

A girl I knew from my work was involved with a dangerous man; he was her son's father. For custody pickup and drop-off, they would meet at her mom's. One day her son was waiting for him on her mom's front porch, and the man walked on by the ten-year-old and went into the house. He shot my friend in the face where she stood in her mom's kitchen. She had wanted to move to Florida, but the court wouldn't let her leave with her son. The court didn't take seriously the threats that he kept making to her son: "I'm going to kill your mom one day." It would be good for our country and our world if mental health checkups were as common as our yearly physical checkups. The National Alliance on Mental Health (NAMI) is the nation's largest grassroots mental health organization dedicated to building better lives for the millions of Americans affected by mental illness. Educating high school students on the basic mental health issues plaguing our country would be great. Maybe we would see signs and recognize symptoms before it's too late. Our country seems to only care about our looks on the outside. We ignore our mental health, and the behavior in our world shows this to be true.

When I was in college a few of my friends went down to the boys' dorms to watch a movie in a rich kid's room. He drove a BMW 5 Series and had no driver's license; it had been revoked by the state. A couple of my girlfriends and I were on the top bunk in his room. The lights were off so it was dark like a theater, and there were other kids there too. The small dorm room was full. The rich kid made us drinks, and I fell asleep, which was really odd for me. I remember faintly feeling someone jump off the top bunk where I was sleeping and hearing a wrapper of some sort, and then I went back to sleep. It was like I was drugged, but at the time I didn't realize this or know what was going on. I woke up in the middle of the night, and everyone was gone, but the rich kid was asleep on the lower bunk. I got up and went back to my dorm room and went to bed.

The next morning I met my friends in the cafeteria, and they teased me about staying in his room. I said, "Why didn't you wake me up?" They didn't know I didn't want to stay, or maybe they thought I was pretending. I told them I felt sore, like he had sex with me. But I didn't remember anything. They all laughed and thought it was funny. I dismissed it and was confused, but I didn't know what to think.

Later that year, his fraternity was rumored to have almost lost their chapter. It was over a rape issue in a small town where his parents' cabin was in northern Michigan. I was no longer confused. What I thought had happened *had* actually happened.

Girls, never leave a girl behind. Use the buddy system, even if she is ticked off at you at the time. Always look out for each other. God made us special to be mothers and givers of life. We need to protect each other. We don't realize how special it is to be a woman. We think it's a man's world. Without us, there would be no new life. We are the bearers of life, literally. That is such a miracle. It is a gift and oh so amazing to feel the baby inside of you kick and move around. You have to experience it for yourself to know. Even if you are unable to have children, to have a child in your life through adoption or family and friends is a treasure. It is like having little Jesus around; you experience the world in an entirely new light. They are our teachers. We think we teach them, but really they are teaching us all the time.

I often think about a married guy, an old friend from college, who started contacting me through Facebook. He wanted me to call him while he had to go through boring work e mails, and he wanted to know what I was wearing. His wife probably has no clue about his dark side. He was the guy in college who seemed so nice, quiet, and shy, all dressed in his preppy clothes. All the while, he was having a girl on the side along with his girlfriend up at school and it sounds as though, nearly twenty years later he is continuing the tradition. He has two little kids, and I wonder how their lives are going to turn out. I said to him, "You are married; leave me alone." I am sure he is not even aware of his darkness. I pray that he becomes aware and gets help.

At times I feel the shadow of my dark side. It lingers, waiting for me to come back. It sends a shiver down my spine on even the warmest of days, but I shake my head no. You won't get me today. Each morning I spend with the Lord. I give myself to Him. No longer do I give myself to men. I give myself to Jesus. My mission is to bring others home for their salvation. I was sacrificed. My life was spent as a slave to men and to sex. Now I am a servant of the Lord. My pleasure is in my peace. No more depression or anxiety. Now it has been replaced with joy—the joy of love and knowing that I am a beloved daughter of God. I no longer feel empty. I have no need to look for love, which I had confused with sex. That filled me up with pain, shame, and regret. I have the love of God. I have accepted His love and forgiveness. I am worthy of love, and my pain no longer exists. Now I am with God and spend time with Him daily.

I need at least a few moments with Him every day. An hour is bliss, but a half hour will get me through. I thought going to church one day a week was enough, or saying a few prayers before bed or in the car—that is nothing. Not compared to the meditation and contemplative prayer, the rosary, and the reading of His Word. I love to join him in the meadow and receive that hug, His loving gaze on my soul.

Just spend time gazing on Him, whatever picture you have of Him in your mind. No words are needed, just silence with Him, your Healer. Don't be shocked when the tears come; that is the healing gift of tears from all the years of pain, melting down your face like a soft, warm, summer rain.

I used to feel I couldn't trust or depend on anyone, and at other times I trusted the wrong people too much. Now I have God. I trust and depend on God. He has the best plans for you. You can trust in that; He knows what is best for you. He wants what is best for you and has a perfect plan for your life. Take comfort trusting in that. He loves us so much. So you can't say, "I can't trust anyone," or, "I have nobody to love, and nobody loves me." You have God, who loves you and wants you to love and adore Him. Put your trust for your life in Him. He will make good come from it—even the bad that has happened in your life, and even if it was by your free will, by your choice. He turns all things to gold. That includes you! You don't have to be or feel lost. Find Him and follow Him. You will have all you ever could need or want. You will have joy and peace to get through the storms of life by having Him carry you instead of feeling like you are on a boat in the ocean, lost at sea in the storm. He has always carried us through the storms, but once in union with Him, you have peace during them.

This book came from God, His plan, and choosing for me to write it—not from me. He has used my past to glorify Him with my story of how He saved my eternal life. I hope it can help you to know you are not alone, to give you hope for a better you, a better tomorrow, and to know that no matter what you have done or haven't done or are upset about, that God loves you, forgives you, and is waiting for you to go home to Him. His loving, warm embrace full of love and forgiveness and compassion compares to no other. His healing is all-powerful and mighty, like Him. There is nothing that He can't make right and heal. Let Him heal you and your soul. Life doesn't have to be so hard. Once you are with Him and become a disciple, His follower, He will make everything easier. Little by little, every day He works on you and your life to improve it. I know, for I have experienced it. It is amazing.

It is why I love Him so much. Why I will forever be grateful to Him. His peace is better than any medication! And it is free! All it costs you is your time.

You will lose something, though. You will lose your old life. You will give up what you think you love. I thought I loved sex. All of that ran my life. That was the addict in me stopping at all those bus stops. Now someone else is driving my bus—someone healthy, someone who has peace and joy and refuses to take that old route ever again. I got out of the driver's seat and handed the control over to our Lord. He said in that still voice, I've got it from here, kid. Go relax and heal your soul. I am His beloved child. Do you believe you are, too? He has a plan and a purpose for your life that you can't begin to imagine. It is far greater than you could come up with. He has gifts in you that haven't begun to be unlocked. You are a mystery that you have not yet solved. The Lord is the key to unlocking that door to the purposeful life waiting for you. What are you waiting for? You have tried so many things. Why not try Him? Once you are with Him, there is no going back. You won't want to.

For my entire life I trusted people at the beginning of relationships who were not trustworthy, until I got burned by their fire. I never had them earn my trust. I freely gave of myself like a child does. Not just once, but nearly every time. I thought everyone will do and think as I do. The ones I attracted counted on this. They took advantage of this and saw me as meek, as a wolf looks at a sheep. But they didn't know, nor did I, that I have strength and courage in Christ. He fights my battles and ultimately wins all things for my good. Because I love Him, He does this for me. I was waiting for a man to save me, not knowing I needed Jesus Christ to save me. If I had to go through all of this to have Him as my brother, then I am grateful for my past. It keeps me close to Him. I don't feel angry any longer at the men I was involved with. Some were very controlling and mean at times. I pray for them and bless them that they will find God and that He can turn them from ashes to gold the same way He did for me. I know in their own way most thought they loved me, just as I thought I loved them.

NARCISSISM

Sixteen

OUT OF THE SHADOWS

"For where two or three are gathered together in my name, there I am in the midst of them."

Matthew 18:20

God taught me to love, to forgive, and to surrender. He gave me peace. He works on me every day to become a better person. He has done so much work on me yet has so much more to do. He blesses me every day in some way. He always has, and now I am open to see it and have gratitude for it. His love is a calm, safe haven. It is a warm sweet embrace, so sweet. I love Him and adore Him. All the fear and anxiety that consumed me is barely a memory. I know I lived that way. I can't believe I endured it for so long. If you don't change who you are and get the healthy person to drive the bus, your addict or habit will continue to ruin your life. Just as I attracted emotionally abusive men, you won't see it or it will be too hard to fight the attraction if you don't take steps to get healthy. You need to remove the blinders and become aware. I would rather live my life alone than with someone who is going to put me down instead of build me up. I don't want to be an insecure woman, so love sick she will take on any man who gives her attention. When you live in darkness, you will attract others who also live in darkness.

People of the light attract others of the light. Seek the Lord for healing and get into the path of the light.

Sex is not worth the anxiety and depression and up-and-down roller coaster of emotions that come with it. God's peace and joy override it. Until you get perspective and step away and out of it, you won't see it that way. You are numb. You can't imagine life without sex. Sex seems to be the most important thing to you at times. It can consume you at moments. It is an empty hole you have in your soul. While some fill it up with food, alcohol, drugs, gaming, or going to the casino or the mall, you fill it up with sex. You don't tell anyone, though, because you know you can't talk about it. People don't understand the disease of sex addiction the same way they do drinking or gambling or food addictions. So you keep it hidden. Nobody knows. Your morals and values that everyone thinks you have don't match up with your actions. It's a hidden secret out there in the world of such a huge proportion. Sometimes it gets medicated through working. If I worked a ton and stayed busy, then I wouldn't think about it. Or I could keep it at bay until I got home. Masturbation becomes the choice for many. It is quick, easy, and seems to hurt nobody. So you think. You don't realize you are hurting yourself. Think of all you could accomplish without having the demon of sex on your brain all the time. The first book my counselor had me read on sex addiction was *Out of the Shadows*, by Patrick Carnes. It is a book on understanding sex addiction. On September 11, 2013, I was volunteering at Grace Centers of Hope, cleaning up yards. They house homeless people and have a plan within three years to help them and for some to even acquire a house with a twenty year loan through them. They even help addicts and help people recover and look for jobs, and they offer day care. It is an amazing program—one I wish could be adopted in every major city. They have bought a few blocks worth of foreclosed homes and fixed them up near their main facility. The first-year people have to stay at the main campus, the second year they live in a house with other people in the program, and the third year some are able to purchase a home. It all depends on how well they do in the program. They are helping people turn their lives around and giving them a chance—as well as fixing up the houses in the inner city. Part of the requirement is that the people must attend their church service twice a week, Wednesdays and Sundays. While I was volunteering by doing yard work at one of their houses, I got poison ivy on my arm. I went to a nearby pharmacy. They didn't have anything to help me and advised me to walk to another pharmacy a few blocks away. They gave me the general directions and the name, and I started walking that way.

I was stopped at a corner waiting, for the light to change, when I started talking to a man, asking him if he knew where the pharmacy was that I was looking for. It was hot that day, nearly one hundred degrees, and he had a tank top on. The first thing I noticed was a huge Star of David tattoo on his arm, so I knew he was Jewish. He said he wasn't from around there, that he was from another nearby city, and that he had been gone for twelve years. We started walking and talking toward where I thought the pharmacy was. He told me he was at a three-quarter house and he was an addict. I told him I was a recovered addict. He told me that he had read the book *Out of the Shadows* by Patrick Carnes, and I said I had read that book, too. Yet, we never told each other what our addiction was. With the title of that book exchanged, we didn't have to. I mentioned *The Road Less Traveled*, and he said he had read that book, too. I asked if I could pray over him, and he said sure, and he told me his name was Carl. That was my grandfather's name.

We stopped right there on the sidewalk, and after I prayed over him. He grabbed my arm just above where my poison ivy was and said, "You mentioned light and staying in the path of the light. We are both of the light, and light attracts the light." He said, "I am a descendant of Abraham, Isaac, and Jacob." He told me I was like Moses and that I reflected God's light and he enunciated the Hebrew word *Ohr Emet* and said it meant "True Light." We hugged and I started back in the direction I came from. I turned around when I heard him shout out loudly, "Thank you, God, for sending me an angel today!" He had both arms stretched out as wide as they could go and palms out, facing the sky with his head back, looking up to heaven. I chuckled a bit and then turned back around and kept walking. But as I took a few more steps, I stopped and looked down at my arm because my poison ivy wasn't hurting anymore and was no longer itchy. It was gone! I then looked up and realized I was under the sign and in front of the pharmacy I had been looking for. My wrist was red where the poison ivy was, but the white and puffy hives were gone.

The Holy Spirit told me in a still, small voice "You have been healed. You don't need anything for your poison ivy." The Lord healed me through Carl. I felt amazing after that. I truly felt bliss, like I was glowing and beaming God's love and light. It was the most amazing experience. For the rest of the day, I was on a high from heaven, and it was like nothing I had experienced before in my life. I never turned back around to thank Carl, though, and I don't know why. I am not even sure if I thanked God in that moment.

A miracle occurred that day, not just with the healing of the poison ivy. Since that day, I have no longer struggled with my addiction. From that day on, I have thanked God for my healing nearly every day. "I, the Lord, am your healer." (Exodus 15:26)

> The spirit of the Lord God is upon me, because the Lord has anointed me; He has sent me to bring glad tidings to the lowly, to heal the brokenhearted, To proclaim liberty to the captives and release to the prisoners, To announce a year of favor from the Lord and a day of vindication by our God, to comfort all who mourn; To place on those who mourn in Zion a diadem instead of ashes, To give them oil of gladness in place of mourning, a glorious mantle instead of a listless spirit. They will be called oaks of justice, planted by the Lord to show his glory." (Isaiah 61:1–3)

While God is a promise of paradise, we have a hard time being obedient for something that we don't get a brochure on—that is, until you have a relationship with Him and fall in love with Him. Instead we take the easy road out and give in to temptation. We need Him, because how else would you say no to all of the temptations of the world? Satan has the secular world right where he wants us. It's not hard; there is temptation everywhere. God isn't very popular these days, and you're a freak if you don't live in the ways of the world. Yet, people always wonder: why is life so hard? We make it that way for ourselves. When you turn away from sin, it becomes easier and easier to keep turning away from sin. Once you sin, it becomes easier and easier to sin. To be obedient to the Lord gives you so many blessings. He helps you with your life. It is still not always easy to discern—quite hard in fact, at times—where He is leading you. Spending time with the Lord leads to the answer in time. When there is peace and things fall into place, you know it is from God and that you are on the right road. You know when you are not. Don't ignore that still, small voice when you get on the wrong path. He will forgive you. Jump off and get right with God. Get right with your life. Recognizing your sin is hard at times, so forgive yourself for your blindness. Ask God every day to reveal to you what He wants you to know and to see. I say, "Lord, whatever person you want me to help, please come through me and do so."

Children do not come with a manual. I realize that, as much as I try not to, I am inflicting wounds on my son. I am trying to be the best parent that I can be to him. Regardless, he will need healing one day. Sometimes children and those closest to us get the raw end of the deal. As I sit and do homework with my son, I am filling out his "Santagrams" for his friends to get from him at school.

He says to me, "You are such a good mom." He says again, "You are such a good mom, Mama."

I am silent, I barely can say thank you. I am overwhelmed by these words. I think of all the times that I wasn't a good mom. Just having these thoughts makes me feel unworthy to have this beautiful son in my life, this beautiful little boy so full of life and energy and sweetness. Then at other times, he is so strong and defiant and challenging to me. He exhausts me, and it feels as if all the life and energy are taken from me. Would I have it any other way? No, not even on my hardest day, for the words he says at times are so amazing, and I love to watch him make creations out of his Legos. I forget about the ADD and dyslexia issues and trust that God has a plan for him. He is labeled with these issues and is unable to learn as the other children do, yet I wonder: why did God make him this way? What does God have planned for him?

Will my son surrender his life one day to his Creator to find out what God's calling is for him? It is a mystery that so few of us look into. We want to control our lives, and then we complain that we are not happy, and we feel as though there is no purpose and that there is something more out there for us. Our egos are so big the Lord can't get to us. There are too many layers of the mask that we don't work at peeling off. We seem to just keep adding more layers onto it over the years. We are empty and void because we have no relationship with the One who created us. He gives us free will and we take it. We take it and destroy our lives with it. We say life sucks and complain about the world we live in. Yet we do nothing about it. In fact we contribute to the misery by complaining about our lives and gossiping about everyone. If we talk about how messed up everyone else is, it will make us feel better about our own messed up, unhappy lives. Do you see? Do you have the courage to face your pain? Do you have the initiative to seek God and to see what will happen? To see Him shine a light on your darkness and find out what it is? What are you doing that keeps you from Him? What does He want you to give up? I guarantee there are things He wants you to give up and change about yourself and your life.

Can you imagine what it would be like to wake up and not want anything? Not want a different life and new or different things in your life? To wake up grateful for the cold cereal you have to eat? Can you imagine, instead of judging people for asking for money from you on the way to the ball game, joyfully giving them money? Even better yet, stop to talk to them, to pray with them. To wonder, wow, if I would have had different parents, could that have been me asking for money and humiliating myself as a beggar? Maybe they are going to use it on alcohol, but what if they aren't? As Mother Teresa said, "It's not between you and them, it's between you and God."

We walk around so worried all the time about what others think of us. We do things just for show so much of the time. We dress nicely to impress others. We do lots of things to impress others. All of this is so meaningless, and we don't realize it. We have all of these idols, and it means nothing. We think nothing of the afterlife and where we are heading until we become sick, be it a true illness of the body, an addiction, or sickness from a failure, like the loss of a job or a marriage, or from the death of someone close to us. This is the point of despair when we are open to giving our Creator the control. For some it is the only way He can get to us. It is why He has us go through suffering. We think life sucks because of our hardships. Really, the hardships are our gifts. If I would have married a guy and had a pretty good marriage, would I have ever sought the Lord? If I hadn't had my thorn in my side—my addiction—would I have fallen on my knees begging my Lord to help me? It was from the pain inflicted on me by my own choices as a result of my sickness that I sought my Creator with heart, mind, body, and soul. The darkest times in my life ended up being my greatest gift to myself and my son and everyone who interacts with me.

I am no longer who I was. Those in my life who knew me back when and are still in my life have said, "I miss the old you." I was fun. I talked of sex and joked of sex. I was their jester, a clown. I made everyone else laugh as a way to hide my darkness. I needed laughter and thought everyone else must need it to. Who cares if I was the butt of the joke? I needed the attention. I was starving for it, like a child who got too much negative attention. It left a hungry hippo in there needing nearly constant praise and consolation. The hungry hippo dreams of awards and things and to be honored in some way. Ah, so this is the key here in our society. The ones who seek money, power, fame, fortune—they are the most wounded of souls. They have to succeed in whatever area they can. Success makes the hungry hippo feel a little better. It is never enough. The wound gets a bandage at the award ceremony or when the bonus comes in or the profits are stated. It is never enough. Their work is never done, and they always want more. It looks to be like greed, and maybe it is, but the root of greed is this feeling of never being enough and never having enough. The pillars of the soul that are damaged are where the sources of healing need to take root. Jesus came to heal for he knew that is what the sinners needed. They were not horrible people. There was good in them, as the sinners of today have much good in them, but they unknowingly feed the bad in themselves, and it takes over the good. It is all hidden in darkness. It is hidden even as God puts those around us as a mirror to see ourselves, to try to see what we need to change. For as you know, it is so easy to judge and see what everyone else needs help with and is so messed up about. Not so with ourselves. The person who has struggled with their weight can look at the woman who sleeps around and say, "Oh, I was a virgin when I got married." Yet the girl who sleeps around may have no issue with her weight, since she only thinks about sex and not eating, and say, "Why don't you just eat healthy foods and not so much?" Satan uses our blindness to ourselves against each other. Our illnesses are our illnesses for a reason; do the work to get to the bottom of yours.

Seventeen

BLINDNESS

"For you were once in darkness,
but now you are light in the Lord."

Ephesians 5:8

When you are not satisfied with what you have, your drive for more is a wound. God expects us to give to the person asking for money even though you know not how they will spend it. God expects you to donate food and clothes and adopt families at Christmas and help feed Africa and your local people struggling at the shelters. He expects you to help because He gave you a different life. He gave you extra to help take care of them. He wants you to try to learn gratitude through them. But for most, we don't get it. We think we don't have enough because we don't have what we want. We don't have what is advertised on television or what is at the mall. We don't see all that we do have, so we are miserable and complain. Yet some people with nothing have what others don't. They have God, they have gratitude, and they have love. They have God and have learned to trust Him, for they have no choice. He is all they have. He gives them His love. His love never leaves us feeling empty and never leaves us feeling like we have to fill it up with stuff, whatever that stuff might be. He fills us with so much love, we can forgive those we once hated and love them, for now we are able to see their pain. We are able to see their struggles. God gives sight to the blind. The blind are us. Not all poor people get this. There are the takers who go from place to place around town and take what they can from the local charities, but that number is small. They too have to hit their own rock bottom. Jesus loves the poor because they learn to trust Him and surrender sooner than we do. They seek Him faster than we do. When you have nowhere else to go, you go to Him, to Jesus, and He is there with the grace to help you change.

In this life, when we live without a union with God, our souls feel it. We may not realize that is what it is. Once you have that relationship with Jesus, you can look back and see what was amiss. I spent my life believing in God and saying my prayers and seeking God in bouts of crisis, going to church intermittently and not realizing my union with the evil spirit that I was feeding. As time went on, the serpent on my soul got bigger and grew stronger, hence the need for rehab. My serpent had gotten too big. There were things I had to understand about my unconscious behavior. Our actions and behaviors seem to catch up with us eventually. We go through life, living the way we want, to justify our defiance to God, and then we wonder why we struggle and have so much misery. If we make these choices out of our mental health and/or our childhood wounds, how do we seek help when we don't know we need it? How do we finally stop the denial, the belief that we have it all under control? In my view, I see an ocean of functioning addicts. The addiction is not severe enough to lose a job or a family, but it almost like riding a wave about to crash into the shore or a bubble about ready to pop. There is so much complaining and misery, with no peace or joy. It seems those words are only in a song. We get used to this life. I feel like one of the lucky ones because I crashed. I wanted to get out of the way I was living my life. Otherwise, when do you seek God? We are teaching our children this. Every generation is getting farther away from any attempt at a union with our Creator.

With every generation, our world seems to be hungrier for money, power, success, and perfection. It seems like a culture of functioning addicts. Maybe I am seeing the world too much in black and white. Or, being an addict, maybe it is just my view from where I have been rooted—seeing all the other roots extending from me that cross my path: family and friends and friends at work.

For so long I ignored that still, small voice. Every Sunday night when I was driving to my boyfriend's house, I would not listen to the voice in my soul saying, "Dawn, turn around and go back home. You don't want to go. Why are you going?" I would start out my week tired and with not enough sleep. I was so annoyed with myself; why couldn't I just say I didn't want to? I was forever the people pleaser, pleasing everyone but myself and my Lord. It is such a relief now knowing I just have to be obedient and pleasing to one person, Jesus. I am so glad I listen to Him. I see my blessings, and I now have gratitude.

"I am the way and the truth, and the life."

John 14:6

He has given us this scripture as a reminder that He is my Savior and your Savior and everyone's Savior. My story is an example of what He saved me from. Yours will be different, but the result will be the same. He gives us peace, love, and joy, and so much more. That may sound like a Hallmark Christmas card, but they are real. I have experienced hell and heaven on Earth. I sought hell unknowingly, just like so many others. I pray for you that God grants you the same grace He did me, to see your sin as I was able to see mine. It did take me decades. You have to have faith in Him and seek Him.

"Whoever would love life and see good days must keep the tongue from evil and the lips

from speaking deceit, must turn from evil and
do good, seek peace and follow after it."
(1 Peter 3:10–12)

I have a cousin who is a Jehovah's Witness,
and she wanted to send me some literature on it
and asked for my address. I said sure, as long I
could send her some literature on my faith. Then
I thought about it, and I told her, "If you are going to try to change my mind about who Jesus
is to me, don't bother. Nothing you could say to
me or have me read will ever change the way
I feel about my Lord and Savior, Jesus Christ."

I never heard from her again about it. I had
been to a wedding reception the weekend before and
she sat across from me. She quizzed me on what the
Lord's Prayer meant, broken down verse by verse.
That morning I had just been at a Catholic2Catho-
lic group meeting where Bishop Burns came in and
broke down the Lord's Prayer to tell us what it meant.

I said, "Let me go get my notes."

She laughed.

So I said, "Never mind. Just go ahead and
ask me."

I did great. I felt the Spirit just pouring through
me. I did call on the Holy Spirit for help to answer her
quiz questions. God is amazing. Jesus got me out of

hell, literally, and the whole healing process I went through had a lot to do with my blessing of being Catholic. Yet, I realize God doesn't see denominations.

Pope Francis said, "And I believe in God, not in a Catholic God; there is no Catholic God, there is God, and I believe in Jesus Christ, his incarnation."

It would be beautiful if my cousin and I could come together to help the hurting souls around the globe instead of feeding the enemy by debating what my level of knowledge is. Yet, if I need to at times, I will defend my faith. I love Jesus too much not to. I am no longer a doormat in any area of my life. I know His love now. I think that is better than having a PhD in any field out there in the world.

"I am the vine; you are the branches. Whoever remains in me and I in him will bear much fruit, because without me you can do nothing."
(John 15:5)

Sometimes our darkness is so great that we need outside help. We may need rehab. There is the obvious addict who can't function in society, as we all think of when we hear the word "addict." But today, right now, if God showed up and said, "I don't want you to go out to eat anymore," or "I don't want you to drink anymore or as much as you do," or "I don't want you to watch all that television or play electronic games," could you stop? Would you experience pain by not being able to stop? Would you crave it? Is it all you would think about? Do you want to stop but feel like you can't, even without Him showing up at your door? What about the functioning addicts? What if we went to rehab and dealt with our issues that we know we have and don't want to deal with? Wouldn't it be worth it to have a better life?

When I asked the receptionist on the phone from the rehab center if it would be worth my trip to Arizona and the money, her immediate response was, "I wish my kids would go through it." She is a humble parent to know that we spend our adult lives recovering—or not recovering—and that we're in need of healing from our childhoods, no matter the childhood, no matter the parent. Maybe we need to save for our kids' rehab instead of their college. The only problem is that the rehab is useless unless the person wants to improve their mental health, behavior, and life.

God makes our lives better because He forces us to deal with our stuff. He gives us His Son, Jesus, to heal us and to bring us to God. Repent and confess your sins. Tell Him what you are sorry for. The key issue is you have to truly be sorry for them. Sometimes you won't know them until you fall in love with Him. I fell in love with Him once I realized how much He loved me. Then in time He will reveal more to you. He is refining you in the fire to purify you. It almost feels like He will never be done working on me. Once with Him, we are in a constant state of conversion for the rest of our lives. A little at a time, He will show you more and more. At first it may be the big ones that stand out. For me, it was the jumping from relationship to relationship. I didn't think I had a problem since I would go weeks, months, or years without dating someone or getting into a relationship with someone. I did masturbate in between the men. I didn't think that hurt anyone. I didn't realize if you think about something too much that it could be harmful to your soul. That is probably your sin. It is justified, and we live in denial. We don't think it hurts anyone. It may not appear that way. When you are hurting yourself, it does affect others.

It is when we are in pain that we yell at our kids more or bark at the saleswoman at the store. There are mean people where the nicer you are to them the meaner they are. I have been around that before, and that is torture. Now I realize they are hurting inside. They are in so much pain that it spills over and comes out. They need help. The people with the most messed up lives, as it would appear to society, are in need of healing the most.

The people who are judged for having five kids with five different men, or the person on drugs or on welfare—they are in need of healing. Either it is a severe mental health issue, or they had things happen to them in childhood that wounded them, or both. Those of us who can function in society and maintain our jobs and make a living, some a very good living—maybe we aren't as wounded as they are. I don't think many think of it like that. It's by the grace of God that we have what we have. We are just stewards of the things we own; it can be all taken away tomorrow. It is not your money, house, car, savings; it is actually God's. Have you ever read about Job in the Bible? That will give you some perspective.

"We know that we belong to God, and the whole world is under the power of the evil one. We also know that the Son of God has come and has given us discernment to know the one who is true. And we are in the one who is true, in His Son, Jesus Christ. He is the true God and eternal life. Children, be on your guard against idols." (1 John 5:19–20)

I found my love! He was here living in me all along. I've come to find out the love of my life is Jesus Christ. I had to turn and face the light. I had to walk through the darkest of darkness and fight my way out of the hole of hell I had unknowingly dug for myself. He loves me, and I trust Him, and I will follow Him for all eternity. Do you want a cup full of heaven or an ocean? Be brave and don't ignore your issues and your unhappiness. It is a call to the Creator. He made us so that we would have a choice to seek Him or not to seek Him. Become a child again and surrender all your pain to Him. He doesn't hate you; He loves you. He doesn't care what you have done. He only cares about being together with you in union as a relationship of deep love and never ending mercy. This is where your happiness lies, in His loving arms. His heavenly hugs are amazing. He is waiting for you. What are you waiting for? All of this here on Earth is just stuff. Stuff we accumulate to make us feel better. But it doesn't last. It doesn't make us feel better. It numbs us, buries the pain, until we think we don't even have any pain. Yet we don't know why we feel so off and out of sorts. Nobody talks about it. Everyone goes about life acting as if everything is fine. It's not fine. Until you know your Heavenly Father's love, you are not fine. Nor will you ever be fine. For this, you have to go deep. You have to keep searching for Him and calling upon Him and seeking Him until you get there. You cannot give up. Never give up. Go deeper, and in God's time, you will have everything you need, which is Him. It is bliss. I was a huge sinner. I had to work hard, but now I am free. My chains to the evil guy are off me. He tries to get me back. I choose to fight to stay in the light. I call upon my Lord and Savior Jesus Christ and his angels to protect me. I no longer fear death. I live this journey out the rest of my days for the Lord of Lords and King of Kings to one day be in heaven.

My spiritual director, Sister Maria Demonte, OP, is a nun from a local retreat house. She specializes in teaching others contemplative prayer. She wrote an explanation of contemplative prayer, and it was published in *The Evangelist* in 2001. In it, she says:

> The Lord calls forth, and many times we don't hear that voice because it can only be known in the stillness and prayerfulness of our be-ing. Here the person is led into deeper prayer that leads into God's mystery. The beautiful thing is that each of us has the ability to go into our hearts into a deeper world where God wants to communicate in a language of love that is beyond words, concepts, or images.

She also supplied me with the twelve "Symptoms of Inner Peace" by Saskia Davis:

1. A tendency to think and act deliberately rather than from fears based on past experiences.

2. An unmistakable ability to enjoy each moment.

3. A loss of interest in judging others.

4. A loss of interest in judging self.

5. A loss of interest in conflict.

6. A loss of interest in interpreting the actions of others.

7. A loss of ability to worry.

8. Frequent, overwhelming episodes of appreciation.

9. Contented feelings of connectedness with others and nature.

10. Frequent attacks of smiling through the heart.

11. Increasing susceptibility to kindness offered and the urge to reciprocate.

12. An increasing tendency to allow things to unfold rather than resisting and manipulating.

"So as not to spend what remains of one's life in the flesh on human desires, but on the will of God." (1 Peter 4:2)

God's grace gives us the ability to forgive. Humanly we can say the words and think we have forgiven. We only know for sure by how we feel on the inside about the person we need to forgive and the manner in which we speak of them, if we truly have forgiven them. Life is all about forgiveness. In this life there is so much perfection that is sought— the perfect mate, the perfect house, the perfect little black dress. Throw that word *perfect* out of your vocabulary. It is the source of so much pain for so many. We will never be perfect. We need to see ourselves and each other as imperfect to have a healthy chance in this life. We will all make mistakes; failure leads to success. It is a part of life and learning and growing. How we react to these mistakes tells much about our mental health. For most who grew up with parents seeking the best for us, it can turn into standards that are impossible to measure up to. The people who cared for us, who expected so much out of us, did so because they were even harder on themselves. It extends to, more than likely, how they were raised. It is repeated, and what happens is that we set ourselves up, along with those we raise, for a life of heartache, a life of never feeling good enough and never measuring up enough. Live your life for God and not the way everyone else expects you to live it.

Maybe the Lord doesn't judge us just by how

we live our lives but how we cope with our pain too. Maybe He judges us by the way we love others. You have no idea what others have gone through and continue to go through, what they inherited or what they experienced in life, nor the scars and burdens they carry. Only God knows all and sees all. So often I have judged, only to end up having the same experience that I was judging in someone else. I judged the girls who got pregnant, and I ended up pregnant prior to my marriage. Who and what are you judging? Heal yourself and work on yourself so you can see with love and act with compassion. In high school, I did a speech on promiscuous girls in the North Country in my speech class. I was angry for being moved away from all of my friends, where I had spent my life up until that point. I was the promiscuous girl in that speech. I was talking about me, never realizing it at the time. There was a girl in the class who was good friends with a set of twins who were my girlfriends. One, I knew, was pregnant, and the other was too, but I didn't know it. That girl told the twins that I did a speech in class and that it was about them. The speech was never about them; they were my closest, best friends at the time. Those twins started a physical fight with me at school, and I would have been suspended, but the popular girls went to the office and defended me.

I was called "baby killer" because in defense I had an automatic reflex of raising my knee, and she was showing in her pregnancy. She had returned a pair of pants of mine and in the pocket left a note, "Don't worry, you won't get pregnant if you wear these." Why didn't I defend myself, as in explain and settle things? I was scared of them; it wasn't just the men in my life that I was afraid of. One of the twins kept her baby and the other one let a couple adopt her baby. I wasn't a very good friend. If I was, I would have begged their forgiveness and explained that the speech wasn't about them. Maybe they would have believed me. I don't remember trying. They weren't the only friends in the span of my life that I was afraid to speak up to and explain things to. I have since apologized to them on Facebook for what happened, but I still never explained anything. And that girl from my speech class committed suicide some years back. I feel, out of respect to her, that I can't explain now. She is not here to state why she thought the speech was specifically about them.

It is never too late to turn your life around. The problem is people don't know what needs to be turned around because they are just trying to cope and live and function with their pain. They don't know they need a savior, so this is why they do not seek Him. They live with pain and unhappiness for so long that they accept it as being a part of life. They have nothing to compare it to. They see the world and think everyone else is happy. They see the world and want what others have. They are in so much pain they don't see the pain in the others; they only see what they want to see. We all have a cross to carry in this life. Do you want to carry it alone or with help from the Divine? It is your choice; He gives us free will. He sees you trying to control everything. It is getting you nowhere; it's just causing more pain. The pain is supposed to be our clue that we need a savior, but there are so many ways to medicate these days that few seek Him. There is so much false light out there. People just don't know, and how do you explain a mystery that you can't put into words? I was so miserable and wanted to die at times, and other times I felt just a little misery, and other times I felt high and giddy and so excited about life. Nothing was constant. There was no peace. Now the loneliness and boredom and thrill seeking are gone. I traded it all in for peace. The anxiety and depression are gone. They slipped away like a boat untied from a dock.

I cannot even put my finger on it, when it all went away. I just woke up one day and noticed it wasn't there anymore. Suddenly I didn't have to worry about what others thought or what others wanted.

I knew as long as I was making my Father in heaven happy, I didn't have to carry the guilt of pleasing the people in my life who could never be pleased anyways. I could stop doing what I didn't want to do. I used to jump through hoops pleasing others, never realizing how miserable it made me. I carried the anger deep within me of putting others first—the wrong others, the ones I was most afraid of. That fear is gone. I feel strong and know who I am now. I am the beloved child of God. I am so loved. I am a worthy human being with feelings, and I am allowed to tell you my feelings, even if it hurts you. Why did I think people could hurt my feelings but I couldn't tell them how I felt because it would hurt them? I kept it all inside: the pain, hurt, and anger. Instead I did other things to cope with it all. It perplexes me how not allowing yourself to feel can do so much damage to your soul. I let all those experiences break me. My soul and spirit felt broken. I had no hope anymore.

I always had hope that I could get that guy to love me the way I needed to be loved. I didn't realize I was dancing with another hurt soul that needed love. The two of us together were two hurting souls. The high in the beginning was great, but for how high you soar you will fall that much when you come down. We hurt each other. I never saw myself as hurting the guy I was ending the relationship with, therefore I became that which I hated; I caused pain. I became the person who gave pain. All the resentment that had built up exploded like a volcano. It was all justified. The rage came out because I had tried to be who he wanted me to be, never being strong enough to remain who I was. I was nobody to me. I had to become them. There was nothing left of me but a shell of a person who was once there. There was nothing left because she gave herself away. I nearly didn't exist unless I was pleasing a man. That is where I got my validation. It messed me up. It messed up my self-esteem and self-worth, and it messed up my life. Thank you, my Savior, for salvaging me and turning my ashes into gold.

When people tell you not have sex because of STDs and pregnancy, do they forget to tell you the most important part? How it will damage your self-worth and your soul, the very identity of who you are? Do they get that part or even think about it?

Do you not know that your bodies are members of Christ? Shall I then take Christ's members and make them the members of a prostitute? Of course not! Or do you not know that anyone who joins himself to a prostitute becomes one body with her? For "the two" it says, "will become one flesh." But whoever is joined to the

Lord becomes one spirit with him. Avoid immorality. Every other sin a person commits is outside the body, but the immoral person sins against his own body. Do you not know that your body is a temple of the Holy Spirit within you, whom you have from God, and that you are not your own? For you have been purchased at a price. Therefore glorify God in your body. (1 Corinthians 6:15–20)

Don't you see the girls having abortions are wounded already from an unwanted pregnancy? God gave women the blessing to be able to carry life in their wombs. The evil spirit gets a hold of them and gets them to destroy it. It ends up destroying the girl. Whether they realize it or not, it is a slow death. We need to get to the root of this epidemic of sex addiction and extinguish it through love—God's love and warm embrace. Men give love, fake love, to get sex. They are not monsters; they are wounded. They are lacking in love but don't seek it the way women do. Women give sex to get love. It creates pregnancies that are unwanted, and children are being killed every day, murdered by their own parents who are wounded souls. We need to tend to the wounded and to love them with God's love so they will want more of it and seek it and hunger for it. The people judging those who have had abortions and who are having them need God's love too. If you want to help, then stop condemning those who already condemn themselves. Start by loving with God's love; we need more love in the world, real love, not lust and fake intimacy. We need more human connection. Which spirit will you feed? Which one will you be aware of? The closer you get to God, the more the evil spirit works on us with subtleness. Bishop Burns told me, "Pride and despair are of the evil spirit." We live in the world, but we are meant to live aware and in the spirit world. We have a guide in the Holy Spirit that we are given at baptism and again at confirmation more fully. Yet, most people don't utilize this guide, not to the degree that they can.

If you think you don't have a story and are not in need of a savior, you are wrong. We all have pain, and we all have things we need to be healed from. Your story will be different from mine, but you still have one. Your pain may seem less or more severe than mine, but it is still pain. Pain from your wounds will keep you unhappy, seeking something until you have an encounter with Jesus. He is free. All it takes is your time and your faith. Go on a journey seeking Him, and you will come out the other side as pure as gold, with the joy and love and compassion, among other things, to help the others. You were not made to see how much money you could make, how much you can buy, or what you can see or experience in this world. You were made by your Creator with a divine plan to seek Him and come into union with Him, to then get your calling and go out to help make this world better by bringing more of heaven here. Apply the concept of buying someone's food at a drive-through anonymously and then driving off to the big version of your life. God gave you talent if you make ten thousand dollars a year or ten million. He gave you this life. You can have ten thousand to ten million and either be unhappy or truly content and at peace and with joy in your heart nearly always. You know the mistakes you make in your life, and the way you have lived your life can all be redeemed.

It makes me sad when I talk to people who think they are good and think they have it under control; it is an illusion. They don't see the way they cause themselves pain or others pain. Life is a journey. If you have sadness, that is often a huge indicator that something is off, and you need help and healing. Maybe it is severe and you need outside help from professionals. The Lord will lead you to them like He led me to the psychologists. I needed a week of rehab. Without my Lord healing me, maybe three months of rehab would not have gotten me to where He has me now. I needed the rehab to point out things like my ritualistic behavior. I never thought having a guy over for dinner was a ritual until they pointed it out. Then I could see the pattern. I never saw what was so wrong with telling a guy off at the end of my relationship, telling him everything I thought of him that I had held in. Why didn't I tell him what I didn't like up front, as things happened? Why did I bury? I didn't even realize I was choosing not to feel and keeping it all inside. I was trying to have a long-term relationship and was doomed before I got started, never realizing that the guys I judged as controlling and domineering tyrants were the inverted version of me. There was so much I didn't see in me because we only see what we want to see. I thought I was a nice girl, just looking for love. I wanted to fall in love. Sex does not get you love. Relationships with sex as the foundation do not have real intimacy; they are like quicksand into hell. I was afraid of intimacy.

Eighteen

PASSING IT ON

"Finally, all of you, be of one mind, sympathetic, loving toward one another, compassionate, humble. Do not return evil for evil or insult for insult; but, on the contrary, a blessing, because to this you were called, that you might inherit a blessing."

1 Peter 3:8

Would your faith be contagious to your children? Father Mike told me, "Faith is caught not taught." Do you expect to keep numbing out your pain in whatever way you do and expect your children to not go through a version of what you go through in your life? We pass things on to our kids. The psychology of how we are made and what we do and say and *hide* from our children does affect them, just as what our parents did and hid from us affected us. Most of the time there seems to be nothing wrong with what you are doing and how you are coping with your pain, since everybody is doing it. People don't talk about their times of pain and the degree of how painful it is. People don't talk about what is really going in their lives and what they do when nobody is around, because they don't want to be judged. It's a hidden, isolated, painful experience most go through alone. It is accepted that it is just a part of life. It's all lies from the evil guy. It doesn't have to be a part of life—to be in that much pain—and you don't have to go through it alone. There are people out there who can help. The word "rehab" doesn't have to be such a shocking word. People do rehab for their body after they have an injury. Why wouldn't rehab for your heart, mind, and soul be acceptable? As children, so much is out of our control; from the pain of that, no matter how great we think our childhood experience was, as adults we turn into control freaks. Teenage years are a painful time for many, especially in this day and age with social media. We carry this pain with us, trying to find our way in life. We are forever searching for our happiness by acquiring good jobs with the ability to buy lots of stuff. Our goal, for most, is to see how much money we can make and save and spend.

It took me until I was thirty and married, with a baby, to start putting the pieces of the puzzle together that maybe my dad was a lot like my husband, and that maybe I had been controlled my entire life. Even some of my girlfriends were controlling, at least the ones I was closest too. It's like God was trying to tell me something, not just with the men in my life but also in my circle of friends. I grew up with my dad on a pedestal and thinking men were amazing and smarter than me. I was taught that women were second-class citizens. I didn't learn to respect myself or make it a requirement that whoever I let in my life had to respect me. Here is the downfall to my life. Without ever realizing how important having respect and dignity for myself was, without ever being taught to require respect from people I surrounded myself with, I gave entire self away. I had no sense of self. I was a feather floating around in the wind, going with whoever came around who gave me attention. Every time, I thought they were my soul mate. I turned into the woman they were looking for. This was who I was in love with? This is who a lot of women are in love with. Look out there and see what we think is important. It's so sad. There are so many others like me who don't respect themselves, let alone their bodies. It's why we do the things we do. It's why we treat our bodies the way we do. We don't know the definition of respect or dignity, and we have forgotten to teach it to our children. It is what we learned—that looking good to the outside world, showing that we are beautiful and have it all together, is way more important than actually having it and feeling that way on the inside.

We wear these huge thick masks, and it's all a façade. We are all so caught up in ourselves we forget to care about anyone else. We forget that the only difference between us and the homeless guy on the street is that we were born into two different families and inherited different personality traits and grew up in different surroundings. I can't imagine what journey that person went through, to end up without a place to call home. He is still my brother. We all have the same Creator. Instead, I looked down my nose at him, and I walked by him without a prayer or a twenty-dollar bill going his way. How I felt about myself showed in how I treated the others I stumbled across on in my life. I judged people so harshly for the way they lived their lives because they didn't live life like me; what does that really say about me? It says I judged myself that harshly, and that it was the root of why I was so unhappy. I had no compassion for others because I had none for myself. I talked about people and judged and compared because it helped to make me feel better for the moment, but it didn't ever last. It was fleeting, and I went back to my pain. All of this reflected my pain, yet I didn't see it as pain. Does this sound familiar?

It appears easier at the time to stuff it down and bury it deep and cover it up with whatever way has been passed on to us by our forefathers. The prideful mask we wear is thick. We seek no help because we feel nobody will be able to help us. Why do we feel this way and think this way? Either because we see it as being too much work, and we are too lazy to go through that much work, or we think we know more than everyone else, and we don't need the help. We think we have it all under control. Then when nobody is around, we are sad, and we wallow in our misery. In the Facebook pictures from Saturday night, we look so happy. We think, "My wife and children will never know about my affair or the girl I am after at work or my chronic masturbation." They are ignored, and your head is somewhere else, off in some fantasyland. You think it doesn't affect them because you haven't gotten help and learned that it does. Your daughter calls to tell you that her husband gave her chlamydia and that he has been cheating on her. But she stays, which is better than starting up with a new relationship, since even if she got out, the probability of her ending up with the same experience with someone else is high. It might not be in the same way, but it will be the same experience. She will be ignored like you ignored her. He lives in his head like you live in your head. But you want to keep this secret to your grave. Your pride is worth more than your grandchildren having a better life. I don't mean a better life because they are smart and get a great degree and an awesome job, the way the world would measure it and the way you measure success. I mean they have a better life because they are in union with Jesus, full of joy and peace and compassion for themselves and others, and their soul will be in heaven for all eternity. As addicts, we are selfish, and we tend to only care and think of ourselves, for our pain is huge and that is all we can deal with. Seeing your children in pain, looking back, you see the life you have lived. You wish you could disappear, and you don't think rehab will help. I don't get it. What do you have to lose? If you want to kill your serpent, Jesus can help you do that. He can lead you to the people who can help you, and He can ultimately heal you through spending time with Him.

I see so many in pain, covering it up with their addictions, trying to keep everything under control. The Lord would unveil so much to you, but what are you so afraid of? Why don't you want to know? Why don't you seek Him? Is it because you think being holy is only for the nuns and priests and pastors of your church? It's not. Are you afraid to give up all this world has to offer? You know you have issues, but you don't really want to know what they are or why. The evil spirit is of fear and lies. We hold hands with him and don't even know it. We think believing in God is enough to be called a Christian. We go our entire lives living with this mask and in this pain, only to come to the end and seek his help. Why wait? Why not do it today? You want a new life and a new job and to feel good. So where are you going? The Lord is the way, the truth, and the life. Find out that He is and experience it for yourself. Your children's, children's, children may not have a lifetime. You finding out today and seeking the

Healer will only benefit them. Give them something your forefathers didn't. Give them a relationship with Jesus. Give them your relationship with Him.

I used to think of myself as an unpaid whore. Now I think of myself as a beloved child of God. I'm remade new. The old self and life are dead and gone. The memory of that life is fading and becoming more distant, so much so that when I wake up some mornings, I think, "Did I really used to feel that bad about myself? Did I really seek others' approval so much that I gave myself away? Was I that much of a people pleaser in pain that I didn't have a voice out of fear?" It broke my soul in two. It left so many holes in my soul. I was being one with the men who I thought were my soul mates just because there was an attraction there. It was a big joke on me. It's not funny when the joke is on you. Nobody wants to talk about the harmful side effects of sex. We have to. I can't leave this world not telling the others headed down my path where they just might end up. They may get lucky like a few of my friends have, but I don't think they are happy. Nobody can carry around all that luggage of past hurts and wounds. We are all in need of healing. It's the best love affair ever, for there is no ending. It just deepens and grows and gets better. Even the dry times, as some faithful have gone through, are good, for you never know when He is going to surprise you. The blessings are always there. You just have to be aware and thank Him.

"For God will hide me in his shelter in time of trouble." (Psalm 26:5)

I get now why I ended up in those relationships. As I said, life is a journey and everything that happens to us and the people who cross our paths is a piece of the puzzle of our lives. Without God, it is nearly impossible to figure it out. God gave me a son who is a strong personality. He looks like his dad and has his dad's strength. My son doesn't take no for an answer, and he is very stubborn. I have to explain everything to him about why he needs to do something before he will even consider doing it. "Do it because I said so" doesn't work with him. I think that is how these children grow up to be such wounded adults. People try to discipline every child the same way. Children like my son get very wounded by having a parent like them, for this personality trait expects children to do what they say and not to have an opinion, and these children are so opinionated. So they grow up to be the adults that are filled with anger. They make great salespeople because they don't give up, and they are so convincing that you need to buy what they are selling. I always said my ex-husband could sell a footless person a pair of shoes. I see the same traits in my son. I used to view my ex as a monster, but raising a son whom I adore and who has his dad's personality traits is enlightening. God is showing me that people with strong personalities are not monsters.

I see now how I got into the fixes I did. The men came after me; not all were predators, but some were, and I get it now. I didn't have clear or strong boundaries, and I didn't want to hurt their feelings. I sent mixed signals. There was an attraction, but I knew there was something about them I didn't like. At times I feel I just gave in. Toward the end, I felt it was the only way to get them out of my life. Why couldn't I just say no? Why did I have such a hard time saying no? It's not always so easy, especially when you don't know your demon, or that you are even up against one. The thing about rehab and counseling is they point out things that you don't even realize. Things, others either don't see or have the guts to tell you. That is the only way you can conquer your demon—to be made aware of the things you have been doing for so long that are wreaking havoc on your life. They are not everyone's normal, but they are yours.

The teachings of St. Augustine say, "Each one of us is given an opportunity to change if we want to." You have to want to. When you are sick of your old life and ready for a change, turn and face the light that Jesus offers to every person. He cares not what you have done, only that you are sorry for it. Ask for His help, and He will lead you down a path that grows brighter with each step. Only He has the answers for you as to what you need to heal and change your ways. The more you ask for Him and seek Him, the more He will become present in your life. This life is not without trouble. With Jesus, we can have His grace and peace to live with joy, even among the storms of life. Knowing how much He loves me and the whole world fills my heart with so much love. He knows I am a sinner and that I continue to sin—maybe not in the same ways as I once did, but I am still a sinner. I get angry at times or fall into gossip. I stumble and fall. I know Jesus understands and forgives me. It is what gets me to stand back up and to continue to love and to forgive myself so that I can love and forgive others. Things still come up in life, as they always do and always will, but how differently I live my life now. It seems so long ago, like a lifetime ago, and really it was but a few years ago. I lived out of fear. I had no voice and no courage. Oh, how the Lord has transformed me. My gratitude for Him is endless.

The only way I can repay Him is to help the others like me, the ones that I understand, those that are in so much pain in their sin. They don't even know what they do is so sinful, for they only know how to survive. Getting through the day with the pain in their souls makes life so hard. They don't know of a healer named Jesus. They know His name, but they have no relationship with the Savior, with the Lamb who was sacrificed so long ago that to most the story doesn't seem real. But for those of us who know Him, who live with Him inside of our souls, we know otherwise. We spend our lives trying to save the other souls and bring the light of the sacrificed Lamb to the hurting and wounded souls of the entire world. In Romans, it is written that it is your faith that has saved you, not your deeds. I don't have to do anything for Jesus. But I want to. I love Him and feel so undeserving of His love. He saved me from my ritualistic search for love through sex. He took my fear and turned it into courage. He took my pain and healed me. He died for me on a cross, and for you, and for everyone. But we deny it.

I never took off my cross, yet I put all of my faith and trust in a human man, a human man I would place on a pedestal, another wounded soul unable to love. I saw what I chose to see in the men

I dated. I wanted to be loved, even if it was a fantasy. For a time it numbed the pain of the reality of my dark, lonely, empty soul. My life is not without a cross, as everyone's life is not without a cross. In sharing my cross, it dispels the darkness. It brings to light the others with similar crosses. When we carry our crosses together, it lightens the load. There is strength in numbers. The more people with courage turn to the light, the more light will be brought into the world to shine on another's darkness. We all have pain. The hard part is turning to face it. The hard part is having the courage to find out the root of the pain and do what you have to do to extract the root. For me, it was practicing telling people how I felt. It was having the courage to stand up for myself. I had to be mindful and practice that my feelings matter just as much as another's. I don't have to bury them just so that someone will like me or not be angry with me. I had a false fear of another's reaction and rejection. It was not easy to overcome this. I would feel so much anxiety and a sickening feeling in my stomach the first few times I would tell someone how I felt. Each time I fought my fear and went through with telling someone my opinion, it got easier. I know for many it sounds so easy.

For the others like me, they know just as I do the pain in not being able to have a voice. For so long

I lived without a voice. I felt weak around the strong. I felt fear around the dominant. I felt like a coward, harassed. I felt anger for myself instead of becoming angry with them. I buried my anger for them. I didn't even know it lived inside of me for so long until I faced it and addressed it. Then it all came out: the anger and hurt and pain. I had so much buried anger that it was shocking to me. Once it came out and was realized, it was like a dam had been taken down. I didn't have the anxiety and depression once it was released. It was the pain of the built-up, buried emotions that were wreaking havoc on my insides. It also came out to the outside world. I searched for a man I thought could heal me and take away the pain of my loneliness, emptiness, and despair. All it ever did was add to it. Each man I tried to get healing from only left another hole in my soul to raise the level and severity of the pain. I couldn't understand. I just wanted to love. Why couldn't I find the love I so desperately was looking for? Seeking love consumed me. I could not seem to get the thing I wanted most in the world. It broke my soul so that I couldn't search for it any longer. I had given up. What I thought was my ending was actually my beginning.

Finally, I gave up the lack of control I had over my life for my quest for love. It led to the surrender of my life and soul to my Healer and Savior, Jesus.

"The Lord binds up the wounds of his people, he will heal the bruises left by his blows" (Isaiah 30:26).

I thought I had nowhere to go. I had no idea I was falling into the arms of the Son of God, who could love me just the way I needed to be loved. I fell into the arms of the Divine, who can save. I dove into mercy. He gave me so much mercy and forgiveness for my past. "For God did not send His Son into the world to condemn the world, but in order that the world might be saved through Him." (John 3:17)

He knew what I had done was out of a reaction to my pain. But in behaving the way I did, the mental illness created a vicious cycle that just caused more pain. He knows all. It was so hard for me to forgive myself. He showed me that is just what He wanted. He had been waiting for me, and He wanted me to stay with Him, but the only way was to repent and ask for His forgiveness. Most importantly, I needed to accept His forgiveness. That was the hard part; since when I fell into His love, I felt I didn't deserve it. That was the serpent trying to hang onto me. The Lord all the while was saying in the still, small voice, my beloved, my beautiful, abused beloved don't believe the lies of the dark one. Get to know Me, grab My hand, and never let go. The moment I finally accepted Jesus's love and forgiveness, His gift to me was to take my tired soul in His arms.

"Blessed are the peacekeepers, for they will be called the children of God." (Matthew 5:9)

I came to find out that, even though I thought I was weak because I spent a life not standing up for myself, really, I was strong in my faith with my Lord, and that is all the strength I need. If I wasn't brave and strong in my faith, I would have never been able to turn to the light and work as hard as I did to climb out of my pit of dark hell on Earth that I lived in. I thought that was the only life I could live. I never knew there was something better for me. I was coping and surviving, and now with Jesus I am thriving.

I am not sure if telling my humble story of sin will help you. I want you to know there is a way out. Jesus is the way, the truth, and the life. It is the same message that has been told for nearly two thousand years. It is for those who want out and are sick and tired of the despair of life that will seek them. Is it your time now? Do you want to seek the Savior and be made new? Your life won't be the same. Do you want it to be? I didn't. I didn't know what to expect. I had no expectations. I only felt pain. Everyone's root of pain is different. But pain is pain. No pain is greater or lesser than another's. It takes so much courage to seek healing for the pain. Most do not. We seem to only recognize the severely mentally ill, the ones who can't cope and function in society. We ignore our actions and behavior. We hang out with people who are like us. It shows us a mirror of who we are, but we ignore it. We judge others, not seeing our own faults. We spend our time focused on the outside and on others, ignoring the pain inside us. We spend time on everything else except changing our thoughts. We feel there is nothing else to do. Yet there is. We can seek help to change our thoughts in order to change our lives. Our thoughts can change our behavior. Our thoughts tell so much about what actions we will take. We don't think of it as being prisoners in our own heads, but that is just what we are. There are dark thoughts that we are worthless and ugly, thoughts of being not smart enough or good enough—we can change all of those. Those are indicators of the enemy in your soul. Jesus doesn't want us to think that way about ourselves. We are the adopted children of his Heavenly Father. He thinks of us as his brothers and sisters. He doesn't want us thinking badly of ourselves. It is not of him. To squeeze the evil spirit out, we need to let God in. How we get to God is to let His Son in, to accept his love and forgiveness, to let the Healer do the healing work that needs to be done in each and every one of us. Nobody is immune from pain or the cross we have to carry in this life. Once encountering Christ, we have strength to carry the cross instead of angrily dragging it behind us. It is lighter when we pick it up and carry it properly with the help of our Lord.

I think of what Jesus and Mary went through. Mary said yes to God and let the Holy Spirit place a baby in her. How scared she must have been to be stoned to death. In those days, a pregnant, unmarried woman who committed adultery would have been stoned to death.

"We know that all things work for good for those who love God, who are called according to his purpose." (Romans 8:28)

It is the same for us. We must say yes to Him even if we fear what it will bring. Fear is of the enemy, and God will have all good come from it when it is for His purpose and we love Him. When I pray the seven sorrows on Tuesdays and Fridays, I am reminded of the cross and pain that the Blessed Virgin Mary endured, and I am reminded that my cross is nothing compared to hers. We are all given a guardian angel to protect us, for that is how much God loves us. I don't have to carry the weight of my sins with me. Jesus died so that I could be washed clean. I can start fresh with a clean slate. I didn't realize I was sinning; I justified it. I was blind with sin.

I didn't see that it was hurting me. He knows. Heaven knows all of this. It's why God sent His Son as the sacrificial Lamb—to let us be made new. My old self died. There is nothing that I miss of my old self, nothing at all. I used to be afraid of going back to that old self. But not anymore, for I trust the Lord. I want to stay with Him and He will keep me with Him. I give my life to Him to do His will, to carry out His purpose, and to teach the others what love really is. Love is God's love, the purist, holiest, most beautiful love. You only have to repent and surrender your life to Him. It is a life you will not miss, a wounded life of misery and despair. Seek the Lord, and He will seek you. It isn't hard. For some, it takes a broken heart and soul before you are willing to give up the control that you think you have over your life. With faith in the Lord, nothing is impossible. For how deep your faith is, that is the kind of miracles you will see, an endless life of blessings and miracles. All these gifts, the Lord wants to give you. The only thing you have to do...is to believe it, to believe in *Him*.

Nineteen

ILLUMINATION

"Jesus spoke to them again, saying, 'I am the light of the world. Whoever follows me will never walk in darkness, but will have the light of life."

John 8:12

"But we even boast of our afflictions, knowing that affliction produces endurance, and endurance, proven character, and proven character, hope, and hope does not disappoint, because the love of God has been poured out into our hearts through the Holy Spirit that has been given to us."

Romans 5:3–5

Slowly, Jesus revealed things to me, and he gave me a change of heart. He healed me of my wounds. He enabled me to forgive myself for my past—for all of it, everything. At the time, it didn't seem like such a bad past. It seemed like a normal past. Many of my friends have similar pasts. Now that I am out and healed, looking back, I see why I was in so much pain. I see how I was living a life of destruction and not even realizing how much I was hurting myself. This is how and why Jesus is called our Savior. I had wounds, and I was trying to stop the bleeding. My medication of sex with self and others had a counter-reaction to make those wounds hemorrhage at times and only made them deeper. I didn't know Jesus could heal me. I didn't know I even needed healing.

He gets us out of that old, nasty life. The life where we are depressed and have worries and want, want, want, more and more, the bottomless pit of hell of wants and never being satisfied. He replaces it with joy. It is the kind of *joy* where you can have stuff going on and start to worry, but then you say, "I will give it to God." He will guide me if I give it to him. He will tell me what I need to do. I don't have to worry about this. Do I forget and start to take things on and worry about stuff? Yes, but then I remember who can help—Jesus—and I spend quiet alone time with Him.

I no longer masturbate. I no longer seek out relationships to fill up my emptiness and to feel loved. I have His love, and it is so filling that I feel it springing out of me at people like a slingshot. Jesus healed me of my loneliness, shame, and anger, and now I just have love in me. I have so much love that I can love my ex-husband, and I can love his mom. I can love and say hi to the neighbor down the street who won't wave and looks the other way. I recognize now they have their own painful pasts. They have their own pain they are (not) dealing with. Maybe they don't know to spend time hanging out with their Savior every morning to become full of His love so that they can wave at me and be nice to me even if they don't like me. I can't leave this world not trying to get out Jesus's message. I am no longer searching for the love of my life. I have had an encounter with the love of my life, Jesus, and He has saved me. He rescued me from my pain. He healed me and saved me from my destructive ways. Now my reward is to run to Him when things come up in life, as they always will. When I have a spiritual attack from the dark one, when I feel hurt by what people said or didn't say or by what they did or didn't do, I run to Him. I have a place to go. I go to the arms of my Brother. He hugs me, and He loves me, and He says in the stillness of a quiet morning, Dawn, I love you, and it's OK; I've got this one. Do you know how amazing that is? It's like being a child again. You know how, when you were a child and you didn't have all the adult worries about keeping a job, being a parent, and paying bills? You just knew you would be OK when you were a kid. Now we are tired, and we are bogged down by the pressures of being an adult. I go to Him. I sit quietly and give it to Him and ask Him to help. I leave it all there at the foot of the cross, everything. For a while, a couple years, I was bringing tons of grief to Him. I had nearly forty years to heal and catch up on. I would just sit and cry; sometimes I would sob, and sometimes there were just these little, soft, sweet tears of healing.

He told me He has been waiting for me for so long. He is so happy I have decided to return home. I am so thankful to be home. I never have to be in that pain again. I can go to Him and give it to Him. He doesn't mind. This is why He died for us. He wants me to enjoy my life and be free like a bird in the sky, flying to wherever I want. I don't have to carry around this baggage of pain and regret and anger and bitterness. It is all gone. It's dumped out, and my bag is empty. He then filled it with love, so much love. I can look at people and see Him in them. I can look at people with love. I can look at people with compassion and forgiveness—even the ones I was so angry at and hurt by. I can love them. He set me free.

He took the chains and bondage I was under and broke them. He got the octopus devil off me. He stabbed my serpent in the heart, and I no longer seek the things I did. I no longer am on a search that will only bring me destruction and pain. I have found what I have been looking for. I didn't know what I was looking for: my Creator. He gave me life.

"You formed my inmost being; you knit me in my mother's womb." (Psalm 139:13)

He knew me before I was born. He has big plans for me. He does for you too. He is just waiting for you to turn to Him and say, "I am sorry." I say to Him, "Please reveal to me what you want me to know and do. I will do it." Be obedient to Him. Don't follow what you want. Give Him the control. He will take it; He will take all of your pain and the things that you do that you wish you didn't. They are there to be looked at as a gift, to keep us close to Him.

Any of you who are in pain and darkness, He will reveal to you what the devil is sugarcoating. His way will get you off the same path with those big old ruts in the road. He will turn your life around. It will be nothing of what you thought you wanted. It will be everything you need. You will have peace. You can't put a price tag on peace. Through your encounters with Him, you will have experienced bits and pieces of heaven, of the paradise, and of the light. It will instill in you peace that one day you won't have to remember to give Him your worries. You won't have them anymore because you will be in your eternal home in heaven on Earth with your Creator. You will realize you have much work to do for Him—whatever that is. It is different for everyone. He created us to do His will. I know whatever He has planned for me is best. Whatever He wants me to have, I will have. Sometimes along the way, He has given away something I thought I loved and was so attached to. He doesn't want me to be attached to anything but Him. He will end up giving me something better, something I never thought of. It is how He works. He takes away things and replaces them with something better.

Even knowing of Jesus and being raised Catholic, I didn't know Him personally, nor did I have a relationship with Him. I didn't know that I was supposed to seek this relationship until Father Bernie told me, "You don't even have a relationship with Jesus". How he could tell, I have no idea, but he was right. I didn't have a relationship with Jesus yet, at that time. I didn't know my life's purpose, as is everyone's, was to glorify God. I didn't know Jesus could take my painful, dark past and make something good come from it. I didn't know how much He *loved* me and that He *could* love a person like me, who thought she was so bad. I didn't listen to the stories of how He came for the sinners. He came for people like me. He is still coming for people like me. Like me, the sinners of today don't know to seek Him and to ask Him for help. I didn't know, and they don't either. It's all about surrender, to give up the control to something higher and more powerful than us, to our God, who holds the key to everlasting life. To trust, to be open to Him who goes against our culture of power and control.

If Jesus can help me become holy, then He can help you become holy. All it takes is seeking Him with your whole heart, mind, body, and soul. My love for Him is great, so great that I am unable to explain and put it into words to the depth that I want to. He was the innocent, sinless man who was crucified for me and for you. I don't have to carry my sin with me. It's gone. It's why I hope my story, not a story in the

Bible but a real story of today's times and culture, can help deepen your faith enough that you can turn yourself over to the innocent Lamb who was sacrificed for you. I want you to understand how much He can help you today. Jesus is alive today. He dwells within you. You just have to invite Him in. He will light your dark path and illuminate all that you are unable to see without Him. He is the key to unlocking what is a blind spot for us. There is a thing that is keeping us in bondage as a slave to sin, in a prison we don't realize we are in, but His truth sets us free. He lights the way for us to get us out of the darkness and into the light—free from pain, loneliness, anxiety, addiction, and whatever affliction you may have.

I have a lifetime of conversion and enlightenment left to be unveiled ahead. I have crossed over, and I want to see my sins and become aware of them. God doesn't show them all at once. In God's time, He will prune that branch and grow more fruit. We will be sinners until we leave this human life. We are surrounded by Satan, the prince of this world. I will always need my Savior, as the evil one will try until I leave this world to gain my soul back.

Twenty

MESSAGES FROM HEAVEN

T he next section of this book may be hard for some to believe. It was sometime in October 2013 that my dog would wake me up from downstairs with an odd barking. I would go downstairs and feel what Deacon Steve from my church would call "the Holy Spirit bumps." I would follow Cooper, my dog, over to a painting of Jesus's face, on the wall next to a window. The first time it happened, I saw a falling or shooting star. The second time it happened, my mind was blank except for the words, "Write the book now," which I felt were from Jesus. The third time, it was the words, "Get going with haste on writing the book." These small internal messages—called interior locutions; I never heard an audible voice—became longer, and I was told in one of the messages to type them directly into my computer the next time it happened. The first couple of messages were very personal, geared just toward me and those who are close to me, but then they seemed to be for the world to read and to know. All but four that I have shared sounded as if they were being spoken by me. With most, I was woken up from sleeping, and while typing, they never seemed to make sense to me. Yet, I would type and my arms would feel so weak and strange. A few days would pass, and I would read them and be shocked that they sounded well written. I came to find out I am not the only one this happens to. I just recently read a few books from different women who have received similar messages—similar, but with different content from mine below. They are from heaven for the world.

Wednesday, January 29, 2014, 11:00 to 11:45 p.m.
A Message from the Blessed Virgin Mary
and the Holy Spirit

She would like the world to know her Son's peace and love, peace and love, peace and love. It's a dark world without her Son. Heaven is getting anxious about everyone. There are so many lost, hurting souls. Repent and surrender now, don't wait. They take so long; why do they wait? They have lost urgency. It hurts them (heaven). The Lord, her Son, went through so much for them. They don't even care. There is no gratitude to Him. None. The world has become satanic. It is full of the dark spirit. He is happy. He is in his glory. It should be the opposite. He does nothing but cause everyone pain, and they are tricked by him. They think they don't need the Lord. They need Him more now than ever before. People won't listen to the disciples; there is too much narcissism. The Earth is a sea of narcissistic people. The egos are too thick and big to be penetrated by the Word of Christ. The seeds planted are lost, blown about with nowhere to take root. More and more children keep coming here (heaven) every day. There is no end in sight to the massacre. The fight against evil is too big. Tell the others about me and my Son. Tell them about our love, about our mercy. Tell them that there is no end to the depth of it. It is deeper than the deepest sea. Every day hug the babies and hold them in your heart. Pray for their souls and bless them. You of all people under-stand the rejection they feel and the pain that goes with that. The parents can't love. They are unable to love them enough to keep them. You know, Dawn, how it feels not to be loved unconditionally. You felt the hatred from a cold, dark parent. It was for real. So many parents need help. Write about the help you got, the life-changing help you got. They need it to become aware to fight off the abyss of evil they are in. There needs to be awareness of the dark side in the new evangelization; people need to mend their ways of sin. Bring awareness to it, to how Satan is winning; in the dark, people don't see it and are un-able to see it. They see what they want to see. The father of lies created that. Make the others wise to this.

Mary teaches how to love. Not enough seek her or utilize all that she has to offer. They don't realize how highly I am regarded to the three-in-one God. I am connected to all three. Tell the others about my powerful mystery. Confession, surrender, rosary, prayer, Mass. Work on the parents so the children will follow. This needs to become louder and more urgent: repent and surrender, repent and surrender, completely surrender. People are so far from this. Who will urge everyone to repent and surrender? Who will listen? The world is running out of time to the end of time. Dark days are ahead. Night will fall and stay night until the bright white light. By then it will be too late for them. The message falls on deaf ears. The world is too loud. We pray for the world to hear and to see.

Saturday, February 1, 2014, 7:00 a.m.
A Message from the Blessed Virgin Mary
and the Holy Spirit

Heaven is not as mad as people on Earth about homosexuals and their marriages. They do it to try to be like the heterosexuals and get away from the stigma that they switch partners a lot. They want to be good. They just want to be loved and ac-cepted by all. Heaven sees this. Heaven also knows God created one man and one woman to unite as one and create life. So what they do does go against God, the Father, and all of Heaven. Merciful Jesus and Mary, we want to help. They are in pain. Pain so great not even they understand the depth, the root, or where it came from. This is part of the evil spirit serpent's plans. God is the creator of life, and the serpent is the destroyer of life. It takes many different routes to do it, all painful for the human. We all have pain and crosses to carry. When one is not aware of their darkness, the evil one destroys their life with it. Destroys the human slowly, killing them physically, spiritually, mentally, and emotionally. This is why we need her Son. He can heal and dispel the darkness within, the dark forces that are destroying God's children slowly, painfully slow, so nobody notices too much. Love heals everyone. God's love is all anyone needs. It is enough to make the world better. People don't believe that or even try it out; there are so many obstacles and distractions to stop them.

Wednesday, February 5, 2014, 1:31 a.m.
A Message Inspired by Heaven

We take life for granted. The breath that God gives us—we feel we own it. It is not ours. It is a gift from Him. A gift most of us cannot see or realize. We go about most of our lives in complaint. We complain about one thing or another, sometimes several things all at once. We worry about the future and hang onto the past. By living this way, we see no joy in the present moment. We can't seem to give up the control. In surrender there is peace, but we are unable to let go and give it to God. We have lost trust in our Creator. Most don't even believe. They can't see the miracles of the divine, for they are blind to it. It is a stubborn rejection of the One who created life. It saddens all of heaven how more and more have pulled away from God. Yet, there is so much despair. There is a busy activity of nothingness, nothing that matters. We worry about such superficial things—our looks, our houses, our cars, how much money we have, and where to invest it. We don't worry about each other anymore. All we can think is, "Glad that isn't me." We don't even pray for each other. Few ask for prayers from their brother in times of desperation. Some, at least, still think to ask and aren't too embarrassed to ask the Lord. Yes, I said the word *embarrassed*. People worry about saying "Merry Christmas" or "God bless you." Really, it has come to this? The Lord was severely beaten and nailed to a cross, and people are worried about offending someone. Well, you are offending him. Jesus. Do you even care? Can you think of it like that? You wonder why you aren't happy. Why should you be? Why would you be? There is no longer any fear of God. It's as if the world is rebelling against their parent, their creator of life. They take no time for Him. Church is seen as boring. It's seen as boring because you don't know you need Mary's

Son. There is no thought anymore of what is good and what is evil. Even if you believe and acknowledge your God, do you acknowledge His nemesis? I know I didn't.

For the longest time, the devil wasn't even a thought. Maybe it is the dark one's plan to never think of the evil one so we can forget he exists, so that we don't realize what we do is of him and pleasing to him. After all, we may unintentionally reject our Creator, but most wouldn't intentionally invite the evil serpent in. Yet, by our actions or lack of actions, that is just what we do. We give ourselves away to him. We have no protection from him. The free will that God gives us is so that we will consciously choose Him, yet unconsciously we don't choose Him at all. We don't ask for His help because we think we don't need it. We want to be in control of everything. To ask for His help would mean we trust Him. Nobody trusts anyone anymore, let alone the Creator of life. We would have to surrender and see things we don't want to see about ourselves and our lives and how we live. It is much easier for us to turn a blind eye to all of it. What we don't realize is in doing so, we make our lives so much harder. We have the Creator of life who will make our lives easier. He knows who we really are and what we need. Yet we won't say, "Father, I need You; please help me." Some of us do. The number is dwindling with each generation. The dark one's lies have taken over the popular population of folks. It's nearly like a Hollywood movie. The villain has everyone snowed into thinking they are in control. He has people believing there is no need for God in their lives, that church is boring, and He can't help you anyways. Everyone acts as if they don't need His help. We carry on in these fake lives, not talking about the struggles. We have it all in our heads that we have to look good, and if our lives look good to the outside world, then we are OK. We don't talk about the pain because we don't want to look weak. It's as if life isn't real anymore, like we are all on camera, all in some show. We can't show who we really are, for then people would judge us. They will, right? That is exactly what will happen.

We judge others from lack of having any compassion. If we had it for ourselves, we wouldn't judge our neighbors, friends, and families. To have compassion and mercy would mean you have united with God, your Creator. Those people are few and far between. People don't even know what happens when you are with God. They have forgotten to see the good that it brings. They are too busy looking good. Most want to look good in their hair, skin, and clothes, or in their car, house, and relationship.

People go by what looks good on paper and to the outside world. We don't think to look at someone's heart, because we don't look at our own hearts. Our hearts are black from our pain and lack of unconditional love. To love unconditionally starts with us loving ourselves that way. We put so many conditions on ourselves to be successful and to look a certain way that we do it to others in our lives. We have forgotten what matters and what is important. We have stopped caring about each other.

To look at the life of an addict, one thinks they brought all that on themselves, just as some think that people choose to be an LGBT person. They haven't dealt with their own pain; if they had, they would know everyone has pain and issues. People would know that we inherit things, and things happen to us that are out of our control. So in life we grow up and try to control our out-of-control pain with one thing or another. When I see someone who drinks too much, I see someone with a lot of pain. When I hear of a girl in high school who jumps from boyfriend to boyfriend, I see someone with a lot of pain. When I see someone who does anything excessively, I see pain. I have dealt with my pain. Have you dealt with yours? Or do you bury it? To say you don't have any is untrue. A better answer is you don't know what yours is. I didn't know mine. I tried to live like everything was fine in my life. Your actions and your behavior tell the tale. To know your issues is to know God. He wants to help us. He wants us to surrender our lives over to Him. He can then help us put the mysterious pieces of our puzzle of life together. Without Him, we are lost. All the pieces are scattered, and they don't make sense. We do need Him. We all need Him. We all have pain. He is the key to unlocking why we have it, and His Son, Jesus, can heal us from it. Our Father is waiting for us. He is waiting for us to return to Him and come back home.

We are forever searching for stuff, for things to make us happy. We search for things like that better job, that special someone, the better house, or the new car. It's just a rat race, and we are the rat in the cage. We will never get to that place of peace and joy that we long for—without Him, without God. Those of us who have gotten there can see the others struggling like we used to. Yet, we can't put it into words to convince them. It is a journey they have to make on their own, in their own time. We can encourage along the way, but to say, "Hey, come on and follow me," well, nobody believes that. We can't see it. It is something that changes and happens on the inside. There are no words to describe it other than that my pain is gone. I don't have it anymore. I am left to watch the others in their pain. Yet, I have no way to pull anyone out. I have to watch them on their journeys of slow death and of misery. Maybe that is my pain. I can't explain, "Hey, it's awesome over here. Seek the Lord and He will make everything right in your life. He will take things away that you thought you loved but that were really making you miserable." *You couldn't see it when you were in it, why should they be able to?* Maybe my story helps—of who I was and who I am now. Or is there judging and misunderstanding? I had to tell you just in case it gave another a glimmer of light, of hope, to walk down the path to surrender, free from your chains. Even if those chains at the time didn't seem like chains at all. I thought it was a rope to climb me out of my hell. Really it was a trap to keep me in my misery, to keep me in the dark, and to trick me into thinking that was who I was. I am so much more than that person wrapped up in that rope of chains. I would have never seen who that person was without Jesus saving me from my own noose. Why did I have to wait so long? Why did I have to be so stubborn and think I had a better plan for my life than He did? It seems so silly, yet I think most can relate.

Once I gave up on my life and held up my arms to Him, my world got turned upside down. He shone that light, and finally I could see how wrong

I was living and how much pain it was causing me. Once He did that, I realized I had a bigger problem than I had ever imagined. I couldn't stop on my own. I needed His help for that too. In my weakness and lowest moment, my life began anew. It was when I realized I didn't have it all together as I thought, as I was tricked into thinking from the dark spirit. The dark one doesn't want me to ever think or believe that I need God, the Father, and His Son, the Savior. The moment I realized how lost I was, the evil spirit thought, "Oh no. This one is waking up from her coma." That was when he began to lose me. The grip began to loosen because I began to fight for my life, finally. My surrender to God could open my eyes to the bondage I was in. The serpent tried to tell me that he wasn't going to let me go by making me think that it who I was. He didn't want me to see that I was more than that. He wanted me to keep hating myself and hating this life I was in, so that I could stay miserable and seek pleasure to numb my pain. It is a vicious cycle; the pleasure is what always ended up causing me more pain. I could finally see that. What I thought was the most important thing to me was killing me slowly. It was killing my spirit and killing who I was.

It was in the moments when I thought I couldn't take it anymore that I could finally give up the control and ask God for help. I finally could see that I needed Him. Once we see we need Him, it's the best day, yet it's only the beginning to a life in misery remade in joy. All it takes is to believe in the One who made you, to believe and trust that He can make your life better, if you let Him. Seek Him, and He will seek you. Let Him love you, and He will teach you how to love unconditionally. All the things holding you back for a better life aren't your income or living situation or anything of the world. The one thing holding you back to a better life is your surrender. You have to have a deep surrender of self into the hands of the One who knows you—the God almighty and all powerful who created you for a reason—to do His will. Yes, it may not be the life you planned. It will be the life you were meant to live, a life with purpose and meaning. You will live a life with peace and joy and a life with mercy for yourself and for your neighbor. Even if you didn't like them, there won't be any anger left or jealousy or sadness. His Son can heal you of all of that. What He replaces all those things with is love. Love for everyone. Love for yourself. A kind of love where all you know how to be is kind. All you know how to live is joyful. All you know is gratitude for what you have and where you are. The evil spirit wants us to stay in misery. In misery, we will seek relief with all of the pleasures the world has to offer. What we don't know is that those bring us pain. Those begin to own us, and we lose control. The more we try to control, the more lost we become. Superficially, we can appear to have it all together, but do we? Do we have the peace that only heaven can give? Not without knowing our Creator and coming into unity with Him.

Tuesday, February 11, 2014, 11:57 p.m.
A Message from the Blessed Virgin Mary and the Holy Spirit

Save the children. Through prayer and fasting, watch over and protect the flock. Please renew the hope of God, our Lord, in young people. Your story will help. Do not be afraid or ashamed to share your story. It is worth in gold the souls that it will save. Don't get discouraged or be frightened. Speak of the love you feel from Jesus. The unconditional sea of love you have been given. It is free for all who love and accept my Son. It is free for those who repent from sin and turn from sin and are obedient to Him. Their heavenly reward starts on Earth. The hell on Earth they are living in can stop. Can the children of Earth be humbled enough to ask for her son's help? Will they listen and seek him? Repent and recognize their sinful ways? This is what the Wednesday and Friday fasts will help with. Through prayer and fasting, it will help to bring the lost and hurting souls to the foot of the cross. My Son is so patient. He is patiently waiting for them to ask for forgiveness and seek His mercy. It is why He gave up His life and shed His blood. Please pray for the world and the conversion of sinners. Sin equates to pain. Heaven would like to help heal the pain of the suffering sinners. My Son can heal all of their open, bleeding wounds. The wounds of childhood have led to the disease of great sin as adults. The Blessed Mary wants her Son's love to be accepted by all, so that His healing graces can be poured out. So many of you are suffering all alone and frightened of what tomorrow may bring. You lack such faith in my Son. You are throwing grace away with both hands. You don't realize what evil you invite in when you do this. You are leaving yourself unprotected from the dark spiritual forces. If you knew you needed my Son and that He could make your life better, full of peace and joy, would you change your ways? Would you fall in love with Him and love Him above all things in your life? This is what heaven is asking of you. The time you spend watching television or cleaning or eating or working—can't *you give a small portion to prayer every day? Why is it so hard? Why does it seem like so much to ask of you? You say you haven't enough time. You do not have enough love for Him. Maybe when your pain becomes too unbearable, you will call out His name. "Jesus, please help me." Maybe you will repent of your sins and recognize how your behavior hurts Him and all of heaven and that you need grace from above to change your ways. It takes such humility to ask for help. It is something the world seems to lack these days. Our egos and the pride they hold are so great. It doesn't seem that anything soft and loving can penetrate the shield that surrounds the soul. No light is able to come in. No love can seep through the cracks. The heart, mind, and soul remain cold as steel. It will take surrender to Jesus Christ to penetrate with enough love to melt all the darkness and coldness away. My Son's love heals all wounds. Love, His love, is the most powerful weapon one will ever have. It is a shield of protection from all the darkness that could ever harass a soul. Please seek His love and accept His love every hour of every day. It will save the world.*

Saturday, February 15, 2014, 8:15 a.m.
Inspired by Heaven

Love and lust are often confused. When one has never truly known unconditional love, how would one tell the difference between the two? That's just it—you can't tell the difference. As humans we want to love and be loved. We are born thinking everyone has the ability to love. We think we are raised by parents who love us. We are wired that way so we can survive childhood. Yet we grow up and realize there is much disappointment and heartache in life. We begin to recognize those feelings of emptiness and of feeling alone. They were always there, but now we have the maturity to notice them. This is when we become restless and start to look for something. Something, though we don't know what. We try many different things to no avail; darkness is always looming in the background. What is the answer? The answer to this is love: unconditional love. The love only heaven can teach us. Jesus's love and His Father's love and His mother's love and all of heaven's love are waiting for us to accept. It is the gift not sought after by many, for they do not know what it will do for them. It is so hard to put into words what it will do for them. The road leading to this gift is different for everyone. Even the road you take once you receive this gift is different for everyone. Maybe that is why it is so hard to describe. No two roads are alike. Sometimes you don't even know you are on it until you get there. You nearly stumble on your gift.

For me, I truly didn't realize the treasure until years after receiving it. I didn't really realize just what I was receiving. I had never known unconditional nor accepting love from my family. I didn't know what I was missing. I just knew I was in misery. I could not live that way any longer. I knew I had to do something about it. I had tried so many other different avenues to peace and happiness. This time I followed the words spoken to me and advice given. I was listening. When God presented things to me through people, I was awake and I followed through. I had His grace to finally be drawn into Jesus's merciful ocean of love and forgiving heart, which was my gift. I didn't give my gift back. I gave back love. I loved Him back. I fell in love with Him. This time this relationship was going to last. It wouldn't be like all the others. This one just grew the more I got to know Him, and the more time I spent with Him, it blossomed like a spring flower after a long, cold winter. My heart had been frozen and covered in layers of cold, dark, black ice. The loving touch of Jesus's hand on my soul melted all of that away. There was a flood. A flood of tears, healing tears that bound up all of my wounds. I didn't have to cover them up with the cold, dark, black ice anymore to keep them from bleeding. His blood poured out for me, washed away all of that and healed them up. Sometimes they are reopened. He is there, present in me to heal them back up again. I don't have to seek anything to numb myself from the pain that they cause me. I fall into His loving, heavenly arms, and He holds me close. His heart pressed up against mine is enough to heal my broken soul.

Thursday, February 20, 2014, 11:55 p.m.
Inspired by Heaven

One's journey throughout life is made more difficult without a close union with Jesus. I never realized being so close to heaven would bring so many beautiful and abundant blessings. It doesn't come without costs. The cost is losing one's life, a life that brought on so much pain. A life warped by lies of the dark serpent. Who I was is a faded memory to me now. It doesn't seem that I behaved that way in this lifetime. I changed so much that I don't ever want to go back. Somehow there is no fear of that, none whatsoever. It's like the person who I was is dead—

she's gone. I wonder what it must be like for the others who are around me, close friends and family that knew me five years ago—that knew me ten and twenty years ago. How strange I must seem to them now. The girl who barely stopped talking about sex, the girl obsessed with falling in love and finding her soul mate, the girl who never felt good enough or thin enough or pretty enough—she is gone. All that pain has been poured away. I have been made new. I have been restored into a healthy girl, a girl who can feel loved without having a boyfriend, a girl who can feel pretty without being a blond bombshell and not wish she had a boob job anymore. I am a person who can now feel—and tell someone else how she feels.

It is so odd to me that we can go through life for so long with such blinders on. I was blind to so much of my pain, not wanting or being able to feel. All I knew was to bury how I felt. I didn't know how to feel it and address it. It sounds so easy to do. Yet it was the hardest work I ever did in my life—the work I did on me, the work I did on facing my pain, the work I did on getting real, being real, and staying real with myself. I matter. How I think about something matters. How I feel about something matters. I value myself as a human being with thoughts, feelings, and emotions. I do. I finally see my worth.

Now I think, how did I treat myself the way I did for so long? How did I let others treat me that way? Like I was a piece of meat, like I was trash, like I was an object to be used? I tried to pretend I liked sex; we can pretend from even ourselves. I did it to feel loved. I was so alone and felt so lonely. I felt so much shame. Each new boyfriend or lover brought another hole added to my soul until my soul was filled with holes, and there became nothing left of me to give. I couldn't give myself away anymore. I broke in two. I was a broken soul. I was so hurt. I couldn't take the pain anymore. I lost the dream of being loved by a man. I gained something, though, in losing that dream. I gained a new life. It was the step I needed into a different direction. It was a direction telling me that I deserved real love. Long-lasting, true love is what I found in the arms of my Divine Lover.

Nothing of this world can compare to the love given to me by my heavenly Lover, Jesus. He knew me way better than I ever knew myself, ever. He got me to take off layer after layer of all those masks I wore. My face is not the face of a whore like I thought. My face is the face of a beloved daughter of my Heavenly Father. His Son believed in me even when I didn't believe in myself. He never gave up on me, even though I had given up on myself. He gave me the strength and courage to seek the truth, to find the help I needed to love again. This time I got the tools I needed to love myself. Jesus healed me, and all I had to do was spend time with Him and want His healing and believe in His healing. I thought all those stories I had heard about Jesus were so long ago. But there are new stories about Him today, in our own lifetimes right now. They don't spread the way they used to. People rely on themselves now and place hope in the money they produce. My story is a story of hope and healing, a story that can become your own. Jesus is waiting for you to come back to Him. The Heavenly Father wants Him to bring you home. You too can be made new. You too can look back in amazement and wonder, "How did I live for so long in such misery? Who was that person?" I will tell you who that person was. That person was someone without a relationship with Jesus. That person was someone in pain. You did the best you could, living your life and surviving without Christ's hand to hold onto.

I don't judge the person I was, for to understand the broken soul, one would have to throw a fragile glass on the floor and then pick up the pieces and glue them back together. Without Jesus, the pieces of glass would cut you and cause you pain. Just as your life cuts your soul and causes you so much pain. This is how most of us live these days—in a life of pain, way too much pain. If I can't convince my own family, how can I convince you? It is by God's grace we are drawn into having a relationship with His Son, Jesus. So I pray and I pray for the conversion of sinners. For I know sin equates to pain. I know love equates to conversion. If I can love the world enough, will I help people to love Jesus and to have a conversion, a conversion like I had? I was a girl who thought sex was the most important thing to her, and now I don't even know how I let so many men see me naked, how I could fall lustfully in lust with so many different men. I was wishing each time that it would be different. I wished that this time he would save me, he would love me, and that this man I had given myself to would take my pain away. I was headed each time right into the tunnel of pain, and each time coming back out a little more beat up and bruised. I put all my hope and faith in the love of a human. I didn't understand what I was doing. I justified everything in the name of wanting to fall in love. Love, the word I had confused with *sex. Love,* the word I had confused with so many dark things. Are there others out there like me? I know there are.

People don't talk of the painful part of sex. It's too shameful and embarrassing. We talk about the fun part of sex so much; there doesn't seem to be any shame in that. Why don't we talk about how dirty and disgusting we feel after? Why don't we talk about how low it makes us feel to have gotten naked with someone only to have the relationship not work out so then we are on to the next person and getting naked with them? We call it companionship. We call it marriage. We use sex as a foundation to build so much of what will never last. There is no hope for it to last. Why are we so surprised when it doesn't last? It's because it's all we know. As a society, it is totally acceptable to go from person to person through relationship to the next relationship and sleep with each person. You are not looked at as a whore. You are looked at as normal. It is what our society deems normal. Yet the divorce rate is skyrocketing in America as well as in other countries. I am not the only person who gets sex and love (lust) confused. Lust equals lost. Our society is unhappy because we are unhealthy. I am not talking about our fitness; I am talking about our brains. Our mental health is declining due to the war on addiction that is taking us over. We are a society built on excess. We seem to only see each other's excess too; it is how the evil serpent works. He helps us to stay blind to our own excessive behaviors. That way we can look around and judge everyone else.

Jesus is merciful. Once you have experienced His mercy, you will be able to show it to others. You will see the world in a new light with a new perspective. I see everyone in need of healing from something, and Jesus is the Healer. That has not changed and never will. He wants me to bring others to him. Those stubborn, prideful people who think so negatively and think life sucks and that there is nothing that can help. These people are hardest to reach. I feel I can't get through. They seem to think they know so much and that they don't have anything else to learn. They are in the biggest darkness. It is so dark for them. They need him the most and have the biggest wounds of us all. Jesus will be there when they fall to catch them. Will they let Him? Will they soften their hearts and dispel the darkness that lies within? All of heaven is waiting for us, just waiting for us to open that door and let the ocean of love and mercy wash over us. What do you wait for? Jesus healed me and made me brand-new. He can do the same for you. I am just one of the many sheep in His flock. There are others like me with a story to tell of His love and mercy. You don't have to live this way, in pain, in darkness, alone, and cold. Jesus is so warm; his love is endless. I trust Him with my life. Now you have to trust Him with yours. Say, "Jesus, I trust in You."

Wednesday, February 26, 2014, 12:04 a.m.
Message from Jesus and the Holy Spirit

The Lord is saddened by the spiritual condition of the world. There is little inner peace among His brothers and sisters. It is due to the lack of faith and following in Him and His Father. The world is dependent on money and consumerism, especially in America. Where America is heading, the others are following. There is no peace without love. Love of Christ isn't very popular these days. To love Christ, one would have to surrender and lose one's selfish ways. It is hard to let go of the way of the world and the love of the world and living of the world. Without realizing it, we are choosing death and throwing away life with both hands. A life rich in love and peace is a life with Christ. Zealous followers of Christ are becoming extinct like the dinosaurs. Hearts are empty and full of hate for people and love of things. It's a long road to nowhere on this path in the dark headed for hell. Does everyone assume they will go to heaven by the mere fact of believing God exists? You can't be a believer and do whatever you wish and expect to get to heaven, can you? It is the selfish person in you who expects and assumes this. It is very arrogant of you to presume such things. You who hate your sibling, you who only look out and care about yourself, you who look down at people less fortunate than you, you who only want to acquire more and more stuff. When, just when, will you be happy? Never, that is when you will be happy. As long as you live without me, you will not have peace. Heaven can only give you the kind of peace that you are looking for to quench your thirst of emptiness. The things you buy and money you seek will lead you to be lost forever—forever in an abyss of wanting more and more. It's painful to watch you fools of the evil spirit running about looking for more of what will never fill you up. You believe his lies. The only way to Me is through prayer, yet you have no time. You have no time to pray and spend with Me. The only way to Me is through surrender and repentance. That would be humiliating for you, wouldn't it? Humility is not something you seek to acquire. You avoid it like it is a disease. You seek to be great like the kings of the old ages. You who seek this shall come last. You will be the last to come to heaven if you get there at all. You don't seem to care where your soul will spend forever. For you feel it is not real and doesn't matter. It matters how you live this life for how your soul will spend the next one. If you care about yourself so much, which it seems you do, then let go of the things of this world and of this life. All those things are keeping you from Me and from enjoying heaven on Earth. All those preoccupations, which do not really matter, are keeping you in darkness and in fear. Come and fall in love with Me. Come and seek Me, and I will seek you. I love you but not how you live your life without Me. A life without Me is a life without My Father. You cannot love and live of this world and love and live with Us. You have to choose; do you choose eternal life or do you choose eternal death? You have a lifetime to figure it out. How long is your lifetime? It is different for everyone. One day your children will not have as much time as you. The time is now to choose Me now, to teach them by example how to live. Every day by how you live you teach them. You give them so much of this world with money and things. Yet, you give them nothing of what they really need or what their souls are really hungry and thirsty for, which is Me and My Father and mother. You give them a spirit of always needing to be doing something. Can you teach them to just be, to just be with Me? To teach them is simple; you just have to acquire the longing for yourself. In it you will inspire them to turn to Me and turn away from the world of things and more of what they don't need, which is just stuff. Loving Me starts by thanking Me for all I do for you and the gifts we give you. You who lack humility and think it all comes from you, you are so wrong. It is God the Father who gives you these gifts that you have. He has an endless basket of miracles for you too, if you would only believe. For how much you believe, that is how big your miracles will be. It is fun for Him to be generous. He wants you to see and realize just how generous He truly is. His gifts are not always of this world. They are things harder to see, but they are there. Every day He has an abundance of blessings for all who seek Him. I love My flock. I am missing so many; where are you? Where have you gone? Please, please, I beg you to come back to Me. You do matter to heaven, no matter what you think. We have not forgotten you. Please seek Us so that we can melt your heart and heal your wounds and bless you generously. God the Father wants all of His children restored and to come back home. I love My bleeding and lost flock. I love you.

Thursday, February 28, 2014, 11:47 p.m.
Inspired by Heaven

Where would I be today without the healing of the Lord Jesus Christ? I would still be in a living hell, searching for love from another wounded soul. Searching for a love that would not be real, a love that would be filled with lust, quickly over, and in time filled with hatred. Soon there would only be a scar left to mark where love (lust) once lived, an emotional scar that nobody could see. Aren't those the worst kind? Those hurt the most, yet we don't know why or what they are really from. If we knew what they stemmed from and what caused them, then we might do something about it. I'm not sure why it took me so long to seek help. What is really frightful to me is that, if I hadn't gotten close to God, I don't think I ever would have realized my addiction. I was told once that when you become close to Jesus, His light shines on your darkness, and you see things about yourself that without Him you never would have seen. He changed me and purified me from ashes to gold.

It makes me wonder how many prisoners of war to addiction there are left back in the darkness where I journeyed from. How many guys and gals are on apps like Tinder, some making it painfully aware that they are only looking for sex? My friend was on there, and she met a man in person through the app. A short while into the date, he wanted to know if she wanted to go down the road and get a room. She didn't; that wasn't her primary reason for meeting him at all. Then later, he proceeded to send her naked pictures of himself, many pictures of him in all kinds of weird positions. Her male friend advised her to send him a text that if he sent one more she was going to call the cops. He stopped sending the pictures. She realized she needed to be more careful about whom she met with. Maybe people are sick of the eHarmony and Match dating websites. Tinder didn't seem like much of an investment in time to set up or much time to scroll through the lineup of men when she showed me how it worked. It reminded me of how quick Facebook is. You scroll through pictures and little blurbs from another's life, yet most of it is so superficial. When she showed me Tinder and scrolled through the faces of men, some looked to have their wives or girlfriends with them, some didn't have any information, and others said things like, "Always up for a good time." It really appalled and disgusted me.

I wonder, three years back in time, if I would have been wounded enough to be on an app like that. Would I not see how superficial it was? Would I be so lonely and desperate for love that it could have been me instead of her getting all of those naked pictures that man sent to her phone? I feel so helpless; what can I really do to make a difference for the prisoners of war of sex addiction? They are trapped in a hell that nobody sees, not even themselves. I do know the pain that goes with that, the pain that keeps the soul in a circle of sickness and defeat. It's dark there; there is no light. There is a double life being lived there. A life where one can be successful at work, and one can be fairly successful with one's family—at least to outside appearances—and one can appear to have it all together, even to oneself. For me, there were not many obvious side effects to sex addiction at the level I had it. Not many think of pregnancy or relationship hopping as a side effect of sex addiction.

It's a slow death, one hidden behind a mask. Few will ever know the real person under that mask, the hypersexual person who just thought they had a high libido and that there was nothing they could do about it, the person who confused sex with love. The person who is passing all this on to their children! Their children will live in the same darkness, taking their lifetime to figure it out, if they ever do. See how the serpent works? Jesus is about truth, and the evil serpent is about lies. Jesus is about light, and the evil serpent is about darkness. Jesus is about life, and the evil serpent is about death. But we don't know what we don't know. Without Jesus, we don't really ever know ourselves, do we?

Tuesday, March 11, 2014, 11:49 p.m.
Inspired by Heaven

To be alone in one's life is to live a life without God acknowledged in it. It is like living in a desert without bread or water. It is to live without hope of a divine power that can overcome any and all darkness in one's life. I lived my life for so long this way. I believed in God and was raised Catholic and made all the sacraments, and I went to church most of my childhood and sporadically throughout my twenties and thirties. Once my spirit broke, I had no choice but to seek God with all my heart, mind, body, and soul. There was nothing left of me. I had no choice but to surrender and give up the control. I wasted so much of my life waiting this long. I wasted away so much of my life on a superficial life that amounted to nothing. I didn't know I could get help for the pain I was in. I certainly didn't know that Jesus could help me. I didn't know that having a relationship with Him and that letting my old self and ways die would bring me such joy. I didn't know it would be the best thing that could have ever happened to me. I didn't know. I didn't know that sex addiction was lusting after someone with a false love, wanting him to fill up my emptiness with his love, which was just lust too. I didn't know that not seeing a pattern in my life would be so detrimental to me. I was so blind. I was in so much darkness that I couldn't see. I wanted so desperately to be loved. Yet each time the wounded only attracted the wounded—two souls hurting, looking to be filled up with something. Love and sex addiction is painful.

It is so exciting in the beginning of a new encounter or relationship. There is so much magnetism that you feel this must be the one. We feel as if we have always known each other and there is such a spark at first, yet it always ends. Each time the pain seemed to be accumulating. It wasn't getting easier; the pain was getting more severe. The breaks of isolation in between just brought loneliness, which over time sent me wanting and longing for a soul mate again. I had so much hope each time that this time it would work. It never worked. It was the thing I wanted most in my life, but I couldn't seem to have it. I wanted to be in love. I didn't realize I was incapable of love. I didn't love myself, so there was no love to give. I attracted someone who also couldn't love. Once the lust wears away, all that will be left is being overly critical, just like I was with myself. Everything starts with oneself. Our ability to forgive ourselves gives us the ability to forgive another. Our ability to love ourselves unconditionally gives us the ability to love another unconditionally. Our ability to show mercy to ourselves overflows to be merciful to another. How we treat ourselves shows in how we treat others who pass through our lives, be it a waitress, a friend, or a close family member.

We live in a day and age when it is acceptable to treat sex lightly, and it is acceptable to have a multitude of partners. We live in an age without love. Most are out for themselves. It's hard to have empathy and to really give time for someone. We are out for ourselves and what we can get. To care about people, we would have to be humble and put them before us, to make them more important than us. That is something we don't have time for in this day and age. There are too many other things to do. There are so many other meaningless things that we forget to have human encounters in person. We get our fill through other avenues of media. Just as a sex addict is someone who runs from being emotionally available, isn't that where most are heading these days?

Wednesday, March 19, 2014, 12:06 a.m.
Inspired by Heaven

Jesus is the light of the world. Without Him, we live in a dark place spiritually. Our day and age is about control. Everyone wants to be in control and control everything, yet this is not the path to the light. It is from our wounds of having no control that we want to regain that control as a way to try to fix our pasts. The problem is that it only messes up our future. Surrender is the key to unlock this jail sentence we lay upon ourselves. Surrender to God and surrender everything you think you know and love. It's all twisted, but we can't see that from where we are. Control looks like the only way to survive our world. It's extremely hard for personalities like my son's. Personalities that are born with a strong will to get their way and go after what they want. He is stubborn, strong willed, and appears to be demanding. I want to say that this trait was nurtured by watching his father. Yet, I think he was naturally born this way. He was never the easy going kid. He always had a mind of his own. It forced me to get stronger, though never strong enough, I felt. I feel my discipline tactics were always two steps behind his will, instead of staying one step ahead. He is hard for me to parent, as it is in my nature not to have conflict and to just get along. With his personality and maybe it is this way with every kid, things never go smoothly 100 percent of the time. So many times I wanted to buckle, but I couldn't. I am always thinking about what kind of person I am raising to go out into the world. What kind of friend or husband will he be one day? Will someone be mad at me one day, like I was mad at my ex-husband's mom for the way he treated me?

For the longest time I somehow held her responsible. Maybe I just had to have someone to blame. Or maybe it was because she acted as if he could do no wrong. I never told her the real reason why I divorced him. I never told her I thought he was abusive in every way but physical. Now I think, "Who will my son be to others? How will he behave in the world when he is older?" If he is like his father when he is older, will I warn the girl who is with him, and would she listen? Families tend to repeat themselves. I feel I will tell him one day about everything in hopes that he will seek help to break the chains and patterns that seem to run in our family. If each generation deals with them earlier than the generation before and gets help, will they eventually not exist? I know living unaware and not dealing with them, hasn't helped my family line. I think about the life of my mom's mom and her four daughters and only son. What if she had told them how she really felt about her life and things she did and things she put up with? Or better yet, what if she had gotten help—help for her drinking? Did she seek Jesus, the Healer and Savior? My mom said she always drank in a cup so that you couldn't tell what was in it, to hide her drinking. I think how valuable it would have been to speak with her, to really have an honest conversation about her life. To know the good, the bad, and the ugly of her life in order to one day have a light bulb go on for me in mine. How helpful it would have been to me and my sisters, knowing how generations repeat themselves more often than not.

It's very humbling to have to tell someone the bad and the ugly of your life, yet it is what connects us. It makes our burdens lighter, since we begin to not have to carry these burdens all on our own. Stop carrying the skeletons around in your closet of your soul. You are doing your next generation no favors. They have to be mature and old enough to handle it for sure, but don't wait too long. Don't wait until they are repeating your life in some way. The best way for them not to is for you to get help as soon as possible. Your failure to address your drinking, gambling, or hidden sex addiction issues—be it masturbation, porn, affairs, or relationship hopping—is just opening up your children to a path of some sort of crutch to have to live with. Because you think you love it is the very reason you need to give it up. Because you think you would never want to give it up is the very reason why you need help to let it go and surrender it. Lent is about giving up something to get closer to God. What if you can't give it up? Then it's time to get help. It's time to get real with you and with God.

He will be just at the end. For now He is a merciful God. He is here to help you become a holy person and be all you were created to be. He doesn't want to see you throwing your life away on a dependency of something. He has way more important things for you to do. You have to get past this first. You have to seek his help. He may direct you to get help with your issue. He will never leave you, and He will help you heal. You have to love Him more than what you think you love and can't live without. It is standing between you and Him, and it is keeping your children and your children's children from the life they are supposed to live. You are not just responsible for yourself. You are hurting them too. The best thing I ever did for my son was to spend that week in Arizona in outpatient rehab. That week, the addict in me started to shrink and get smaller, and there the dawning of a new Dawn began. From that point on, she got bigger and stronger. The addict got to drive less and less. From that I became a better mom, and from that I started to educate my son on addiction without even knowing it. I realize that if he grows into the teenager who is caught drinking or doing drugs of any kind, it's not because he is a bad, rebellious kid like I thought I was. It's because he is wounded, and he is in need of some sort of healing. We all are, but I know now that the kids, the people who rely on substances, have wounds that are bigger and darker than some of the others who don't take that path in life. I get it now. My compassion is greater for them. If they don't have money to get help even if they want to, what happens to them? My counselor told me, "You can heal 60 percent if you just do the twelve steps, and if you just go to rehab, 55 percent, and if you do both, there is a 97 percent chance that you will recover as an addict."

Then you throw Jesus in there and turn yourself over to Him for the healing you need, the really deep soul healing that is in dire need of His love. It takes money to get people to rehab—money they often don't have. Insurance wouldn't cover mine because I wasn't on meds or suicidal. How many others are in the same boat I was in? I have no idea. Maybe it's why people don't even bother trying to get better. I think awareness is the first problem and money for treatment is the second. It's on you to become aware. It's on you to not ignore your issues. It's on you to do something about it. Twelve-step meetings only cost a buck. Jesus is free. Well, He wants all of you for it to work. He wants your complete surrender. You have to want to kill your serpent. You have to fight for the life you are meant to live. Jesus will help you, but you have to desire Him. Where are you with your journey? I'm in the loving arms of Jesus. I wasn't always here. You can get here too. I am so thankful I gave up that old life. That old life is gone. The girl I was doesn't exist; it's barely a memory. It seems like it all happened to someone else...not to me.

Friday, March 28, 2014, 12:09 a.m.
Last Message Inspired by Heaven

Here I am, Lord, a broken soul. You are the Creator of the world. I was born into a family that lived in much darkness. Through your Son, I was remade new into your likeness. You transformed me into a holy person, a person with a desire to love You and to be obedient to You. Much has happened in my life, much I do not understand. It seems I was always asking that question: why me, Lord? Now I no longer ask that question; instead, I just trust. I trust in You, and now I am a child again. I don't need to know why You do what You do. I know that You have your reasons, even though at the time I have no clue where the path I am on will lead me. You manifest Your power and glory in too many ways for me to see Your mystery. There are blessings that You bestow on me that I would never have seen. They seem to happen when I least expect them. How mighty You are. Now I know why the light is more powerful than the darkness. Your beautiful light overcame my darkness. I know it can overcome that of anyone's. I wish more would seek You. Their pain is great, yet they do not begin to fathom what Your love can do for them. I am nobody, Lord; they won't believe me. I wanted to glorify You and Your kingdom with my story of healing, yet most won't listen. Most won't see or hear the depth of Your mercy and love for me as an example for the entire world. So many don't believe love and sex addiction exists, or that it is a painful sickness. Only those who are in it and at the bottom, in the pit of the hell it causes, will listen and want out.

· · · · ·

I write this book for you to give you hope as a way to get out. You have to want to get out. You will have to seek the light and do the work it takes to get to the light. The serpent doesn't want to let you go. He wants your soul for all of eternity. Don't give up. It's worth the fight out of the hell you are in. He masks it with the pleasure of orgasms and the high of falling in lust, but you know they don't last. You will always come back down into the pit. Open your eyes and see the pattern of destruction it has caused you. For you to see it and stop being in denial is the only way you will want to stop being a pleasure seeker and want something real and lasting. God's love is real and lasting. It's been over three years now since I fell in love with Him and felt His love for me, and I don't see it ending, ever. It's the greatest of loves. He gives back. He is constantly giving back so much. He fills me up, and love just spills out of me. Love for everyone. He cuts off the bad parts of me and replaces them with good, healthy parts, producing life. Fall in love. Fall in love with your Creator. He is waiting for you to come back to Him. He is waiting for you to come back home. All of heaven's arms are open wide waiting for the lost sheep to return to the Shepherd. The lost sheep is you. You who hurt and who are broken and looking for something—it is God you crave. All the things of this world can't give you peace and love. They are of the evil one. You won't miss what you think you love. You will be so grateful to be out of it and away from it.

You don't realize it is costing you your life, your soul. It is costing not just yours but your children's also. You are such an example to them. With everything you do, they are watching you. You teach them with everything you say and do every time you are around them. They will be like you, or they will attract a mate with traits similar to yours. Who do you want them to be, and who do you want them to be with? You are setting the stage for their future. Don't delay your heavenly love affair. It is time. The time is now to seek healing, to confess your sins, and to be free of the evil within. Jesus is your friend. Speak with Him and surrender to Him. He can help you get close to Him. Increase your desire for Him, and He will increase His desire for you. Begin to want to want Him. He only knows love and peace, and that is just what you will get from Him: love and peace, peace and love. Your darkness and emptiness will have no more room in your soul to live. There will only be room for Jesus's peace and love from heaven. It's for everyone. Stop living your life in the darkness. Do not be afraid of God's light. He will heal everything you discover about yourself that is of the darkness. Become a big, bright light for all to see. Shine with your Creator's love and peace. Once you have it, you have it for all eternity.

"I love you, Lord, my strength" (Psalm 18:2).

God loves each of us as if there were only one of us.
—St. Augustine

Works Cited

WWW.ASAM.ORG/FOR-THE-PUBLIC.
Short Definition of Addiction.
American Society of Addiction Medicine. 2015.

• • • • •

WWW.PYSCHGUIDES.COM/GUIDES/SEX-AD-
DICTION-SYMPTOMS-CAUSE-AND -EFFECTS/

• • • • •

NAB The New Cathholic Answer Bible. Fireside
Catholic Publishing.

• • • • •

WWW.AUSTINLEARNINGSOLUTIONS.COM
2010-2015.

Made in the USA
Charleston, SC
21 February 2017